A WALK
IN THE
CLOUDS

A WALK
IN THE
CLOUDS

FIFTY YEARS AMONG THE MOUNTAINS

KEV REYNOLDS

BEAUFORT
BOOKS

Originally published in the UK by Cicerone
2 Police Square, Milnthorpe, Cumbria LA7 7PY www.cicerone.co.uk

Library of Congress Cataloging-in-Publication Data
Reynolds, Kev.
A walk in the clouds : fifty years among the mountains / Kev Reynolds.
pages cm
Includes bibliographical references and index.
ISBN 978-0-8253-0732-4 (alk. paper)
1. Reynolds, Kev. 2. Mountaineers--Europe--Biography. 3. Mountaineers--
Africa--Biography. I. Title.
GV199.92.R496A3 2014
796.522092--dc23
[B]
2013039175

All photographs are by the author unless otherwise stated.

For inquiries about volume orders, please contact:

Beaufort Books
27 West 20th Street, Suite 1102 New York, NY 10011
sales@beaufortbooks.com

Published in the United States by Beaufort Books
www.beaufortbooks.com

Distributed by Midpoint Trade Books
www.midpointtrade.com

Printed in the United States of America

Cover photo: Kev Reynolds
Back photo: Jonathan Williams
Interior Design by Caroline Draper
Cover Design: Michael Short

For the Masters of Cicerone:

Walt Unsworth—who had enough faith
to give me my first break

Jonathan Williams—for continuing to believe,
and for his support and friendship

ACKNOWLEDGEMENTS

Camaraderie being a valued offshoot of high adventure, the first word of thanks must go to the numerous friends, named and unnamed, who shared memorable days among the mountains, and who feature in some of the stories in this book. I hope they'll enjoy reliving these times too, but forgive me if there are some they'd rather forget! My wife is the ultimate life support system. For years she worked tirelessly to pay the bills and hold the family together while I roamed the high places in an attempt to become established as a writer. Words are insufficient to express my debt to her, but I trust she knows through the love we share. I'm grateful to my friends Michèle Ravier in Bordeaux, and Pete Smith (nearer to home) for their lively company and use of photographs. Cicerone has gathered a talented team in Milnthorpe, and their skills and friendship are much appreciated. Special thanks to my editor, Hazel Clarke, for her sound advice and encouragement, to Caroline Draper who designed the book, and to Jonathan Williams who took it on and, having discovered that he features in it, threatened to embarrass me with his words of introduction. He, and his predecessor, Walt Unsworth—the "Masters of Cicerone"—have enabled me to survive for so long in the world's best job, so my final words of gratitude are saved for them. By producing literally hundreds of guidebooks in the past four decades, they've contributed hugely to the outdoor community. They also changed my life, and I'll always be thankful for that.

CONTENTS

ALPS • 61

HIMALAYA • 139

OTHER WILD PLACES • 193

PUBLISHER'S FOREWORD

My friend Kev Reynolds has spent fifty years exploring mountain landscapes and thirty years writing about his experiences. In *A Walk in the Clouds* he shares some of the high points of a full and happy life as a wanderer and writer.

I first met Kev at a book fair in London many years ago, when my wife Lesley and I were in the process of taking on Cicerone Press. Kev had come to inspect his new publisher. He brought with him the manuscript of a guide to trekking in the Manaslu region of the Himalaya to see whether we would publish it. Naturally we did and we have carried on doing the same slightly crazy thing ever since.

Over the years, we have shared many days and weeks in the hills, whether in the Alps or the Himalaya, Cumbria or Kent. There have been whole days poring over maps and debating how best to bring new mountain areas to life for walkers, trekkers, and mountaineers.

Kev is the leading authority on many mountain ranges, including the Pyrenees, many regions of the Alps, and the Nepal Himalaya. As the author of numerous guides he has inspired many thousands of trekkers to explore some of the most beautiful parts of the planet. As a lecturer in the dark winter months, he regularly evokes the mood and majesty of the mountains to spellbound audiences.

In this book Kev tells how he set off, aged 21, to explore the Atlas Mountains of Morocco—and never looked back. He abandoned his desk-bound local government job to pursue a life in the mountains, living and working in Britain, Austria, and Switzerland before finding his true metier as a writer.

Kev's first book, *Walks and Climbs in the Pyrenees*, came out in 1978. Now in its fifth edition, it is still regarded as the definitive guide to the range, even by many French experts. Since then Kev has written 37 books and guides with Cicerone, and 14 with other publishers, and written widely for other books and magazines.

Even today, Kev is always looking for new places to explore as recent trips to Ladakh and the newly-opened Mugu region of western Nepal attest.

To those who know him, Kev is one of the world's natural and great gentlemen. He is always positive, ready to help, and a true friend and great family man. To the rest of the trekking world, he is our leading guide. Few tributes can match the question often heard around an alpine hut in the early evening from trekkers pondering the next day's challenge or looking back, tired but happy, on excitements just experienced and those to come: "So . . . what does Kev say?"

JONATHAN WILLIAMS

We all have these moments, moments as big as years,
when we experience something so powerful or profound
that, although it may last for only a very short time,
it can be recalled decades later in all its vivid intensity.

All I know is that life is an adventure and
we must cherish every moment to live it to the full.

A WORD BEFORE WE BEGIN

We all have these moments, moments as big as years, when we experience something so powerful or profound that, although it may last for only a very short time, it can be recalled decades later in all its vivid intensity. Life is full of them—moments of humor, excitement, adventure; moments of drama, relief, and inspiration; moments that prove to be life-changing, life-enhancing and uplifting; and moments of quiet contemplation in the midst of wild nature. They mold our character and make us who we are.

This book is a treasure trove of such moments harvested from fifty years among the mountains. There are no tales of gripping adventure on the world's highest or most challenging peaks, nor are there accounts of horrendous accidents—I leave such stories for those at mountaineering's sharp end. My climbs have been modest but exhilarating, and I have discovered, on reflection, that it is not often the summits themselves that stand out as highlights of my career. It's the experiences won on and around the mountains that count.

Of course, days among mountains are not all blessed with sunshine. Clouds, whether they be drifting innocently across the summits or preludes to a storm, form an integral part of the mountain landscape, adding both movement and mystery.

My long walk among such clouds has left me with a rich store of memories. This collection is a celebration of wild places in all their seductive mystery—a commemoration of mountains and valleys;

friends with whom some great days have been shared; people met along the way; the generosity of strangers; humor plucked from the most unlikely situation. A celebration of life. If there's one recurring theme, it's the sheer joy of being "out there." The mountain world confronts all who enter it with a reality at odds with that of everyday living. In wild places the ordinary becomes extraordinary.

Although this is an autobiographical collection, it's by no means an autobiography. Some of the locations for these stories have been identified and the same goes for the friends who shared and enriched many of these experiences. A few are mentioned by their first name; a tiny minority have been given a different identity to avoid embarrassment.

There's no chronological order to follow. This is not a book where you need to start at the beginning and work your way through to the end, so I'd suggest you open at any page and take pot luck.

Memory is like that, too—it doesn't work to an orderly schedule. One of my favorite authors, John Stewart Collis, once likened the power of memory to a journey taken through "the unboundaried kingdom of the mind." That's how this book developed. Being something of an insomniac I often lie awake for several hours during the night experiencing once again days of high living—not as a nostalgic trek down memory lane, but as a spur to creating more such memories for the future.

For perhaps the first time in one of my books, my wife is referred to as "Min." It's not her real name, but it's how she's known. When we share long mountain trips we both keep journals and read them to one another months later. As we do, we're constantly astonished at the differences. Written at the end of each day, either curled up in a tent or in a quiet corner of a mountain hut, we recall the happenings of that day with such contrasting emphasis that you'd think we'd been on different journeys. I have a loft creaking with the weight of these journals, but even so some memories are mysteriously absent from their pages—yet they come to me unbidden as fresh as the day they occurred.

Memory may play tricks, perhaps. All I know is that life is an adventure and we must cherish every moment to live it to the full.

KEV REYNOLDS
Froghole, Spring 2013

ATLAS MOUNTAINS

Exotic Mountain Playground

Reaching altitudes of over 13,000 feet, the Atlas Mountains stretch across the shoulder of northwest Africa from western Morocco to Tunisia. Wild, rugged, and easily accessible from Marrakech, today the highest summits and the valleys that radiate from them have become a popular destination for European climbers and trekkers, for whom they represent the nearest exotic mountain playground.

Having served an apprenticeship climbing mostly in north Wales, the Lake District, and Scotland, the Atlas were my first "big" mountains when I went there with an expedition in 1965. Apart from the Berber inhabitants we met in the valleys, and the odd goatherd in surprisingly remote places, we had them to ourselves. There were no commercial trekking companies in those days, and it would be another 15 years before the first English-language guidebook appeared. Cheap flights were unknown, and we made our journey to and from Morocco through France and Spain on the back of a three-ton ex-army truck.

That journey was an adventure in itself. But it was the mountains, and experiences won there, that had the greatest impact on me. They changed my life. We climbed all and everything that appealed, crossed cols and visited remote valleys and villages, and on one of the 13,000 foot summits I made two decisions which, on reflection, seemed incompatible. The first was to marry my girlfriend, and the second was to abandon the job in which I was working Monday to Friday, looking forward to Saturday, and try to find work among mountains. Nearly fifty years on, I have no reason to regret either decision.

Exactly twenty-one years after that first visit, I returned as a journalist to accompany a trekking party making a tour of the central block of the High Atlas. In the decades between those two visits the mountains appeared to have changed very little. But my life had been transformed.

TRAVELS IN AN ANCIENT LAND

1965: At 21 I was wide-eyed and eager for adventure, and the Atlas Mountains were seductive in their wild mystery—so different from anything I'd known before. With fitness and misplaced confidence rather than any natural ability, we climbed with naïve ambition— yet we survived. But perhaps more than any vertical activity, it was the journeys made to distant valleys that held the greatest appeal and which now come alive more vividly in the memory.

This land seemed to belong to the Old Testament. It felt culturally ancient, part of another world. Sun-baked and barren in summer, it had rock-strewn canyons where goats searched for something on which to graze. From the summits of snow-free mountains that filled every horizon, a golden haze told of the Sahara. There were no reminders of the twentieth century, and the dreamy-eyed goat-herd who stood at the edge of our camp each morning could have been descended from Abraham.

Under his gaze three of us left our tents behind, and with ruck-sacks packed for a few days of exploration climbed towards the head of the valley, bore left to cross a 11,000 foot pass, then fought a way down the other side among a turmoil of rocks and boulders through which a mule-trail unraveled into an arid gorge. In its bed waist-high thistles were the only signs of vegetation, and apart from mule dung and the black pebbles of goat droppings nothing broke the monotony of rust-colored stone. As cliffs hemmed us in, our voices spoke back at us in echoes that hung for long moments in the air before being vanquished by the clatter of rock upon rock.

Late in the day we turned a spur to discover, clinging to the hillside like a series of swallows' nests, a village of flat-roofed houses commanding a wonderland of terraced fields and groups of trees. The silver of overflowing irrigation ditches flashed in the sunlight; on a level with the village, and all below it, the mountain slope was vibrantly green and fertile; above the houses, bare crags offered a stark contrast.

At the foot of the terraces a small rectangular meadow was overhung by a walnut tree and outlined by drystone walls. The grass had been cropped short and a waterless ditch ran through the middle. Nearby, two barefooted girls stood and stared; one had an open sore on her cheek troubled by flies. She turned to her friend; they both giggled, then scampered up the path to the village.

We sat beneath the tree as the sun slid behind the mountains, chasing shadows through the valley and up the hillside to smother the houses one by one. The girls returned, bringing with them older siblings and three or four adults, with whom we exchanged greetings and shook hands. With no common words between us, pantomime was used to request permission to sleep in the meadow. The Berbers, we had found on our first day in the mountains, were hospitable, if openly inquisitive, and the villagers here confirmed those early impressions. We were welcome to spend the night in their meadow, but we couldn't expect privacy.

Darkness fell, and as we prepared a simple meal more villagers came down to join us. Someone hung a lantern in the tree while several children crouched in the branches, the better to see what we were up to. Adults either leant or sat upon the wall; Berber voices discussed our basic culinary skills; a jug of milk was placed beside us—a simple gift for strangers.

As the valley was chorused by cicadas, cigarettes were handed round. Some fingers greedily took more than one, the spares being secreted inside the folds of a *djellaba*, and for the next few minutes faces momentarily glowed as lips drew in the nicotine and inhaled.

Eventually the villagers either grew bored with us or decided it was time to eat, for they deserted us in small groups and went back up the stony path to their houses. The lantern was left in the tree for our use, and up in the village candlelight flickered behind glass-free windows.

It was too warm to use a sleeping bag, so I lay on mine gazing at the stars, playing and replaying moments of the day, urging myself to forget nothing, to soak it all up and store it away. Here in an Old Testament land I was aware of creating memories for unknown tomorrows.

Sleep was blissfully elusive, and long after the village had fallen silent and the cicadas were hushed, a faint sound of music came drifting on the balmy night air. The music, the beating of flat drums and voices singing, grew louder, drifting along an unseen pathway high above the valley bed. It reached the houses, where lanterns showed revellers home from a wedding. Shadows revealed figures dancing on rooftops; the drumbeat, the singing voices, the odd explosion of laughter, all these sounds built to a pitch . . . then silence broke like a wave over the valley. Lights went out. It was midnight.

In the morning, shortly after dawn, we were rudely woken by water seeping across our sleeping bags. A stone had been removed from an irrigation ditch upstream of our bivvy site, and now we found ourselves lying in a water meadow.

Finding himself taking an involuntary cold bath, Mike swore, then broke into laughter. Wet sleeping bags hardly mattered. It was time to get up, dry off, and move on.

MULES, FROGS, AND BIVVY BAGS

Twenty-one years after that first visit I found myself drawn again to the Atlas Mountains, this time with a trekking party; my commission was to write a piece about the experience for a magazine. Exactly twice as old as I'd been on that first visit, I was well aware that my enthusiasm for mountain travel had not dimmed in the slightest, and Morocco's high places were every bit as rewarding as they had been in 1965.

It was a good hour or so before the mules caught up. We were making the most of the shade cast by a solitary juniper tree not 6 feet high when we saw them. Mules first, and behind came the muleteers striding in cream-colored *djellabas* and home-made sandals with Michelin-tread soles; around them hung the Atlas smell of warm leather and fresh dung mingled with dust that rose in low clouds disturbed by 16 shod hooves. The lead mule halted. The others stopped too, snorting and shaking their manes that set bells tinkling until a well-aimed stone and a whistle through closed teeth from Ibrahim got them moving again. I stood up and followed at a discreet distance, hoping to avoid a lungful of that dust.

It was better on the pass—the air a little cooler, with a vague breeze flowing across scrub-pocked slopes—but a summer haze restricted views beyond the second of what I imagined would be countless ridges before the mountains fell on the edge of the desert. I thought I could smell rain. Ten minutes later the first drops fell, so large and well spaced that you could actually count them as they made damp craters in the trail, the edges of which collapsed inwards the instant they dried. A few rumbles of thunder could be heard behind us, muffled by summits nearly 13,000 feet high. Not wanting to be caught here by the storm, we headed down into the misting valley, the mules forging ahead, muleteers holding onto tails, talking all the while.

There was no more thunder, but it rained all the way down. Not the heavy rain predicted by those initial forerunner drops on the pass, but a steady, persistent drizzle that soaked shirts and steamed glasses. Too warm to bother with rain gear, wet clothing was acceptable, but towards evening, once we'd chosen a site for our bivouac on a meadow where two streams met at a confluence of valleys, dry shirts and anoraks were put on and we began to prepare a meal.

Rain continued to fall while the meal was cooked. Clouds lowered over the mountains and brought an early nightfall. It rained while we ate, and it was still raining when we slid into bivvy bags beneath a star-free sky. Frogs slipped into the water and eyed their new neighbors from a low vantage point.

The mules were hobbled for the night, but you could hear their teeth tearing at the short grass, followed by the unmistakable sound of digestive tracts gurgling and the odd fart too close for comfort. I made a mental note not to sleep near a mule again.

Our bivvy site was a rarity in this corner of the Atlas Mountains—it consisted of soft, fairly level turf and a pair of meandering streams. Wild mint grew along the margins of one; tall thistles with bulbous heads stood in clumps alongside the other. There was no village, so no terracing or ditches for irrigation on the hillsides; no trees nor shrubs, but a half-circular wall of rocks about knee-high suggested there had once been a shelter here—perhaps for a shepherd.

Headtorches went out one by one, and at last even the voices of the muleteers fell silent. Yet sleep was elusive. Lying there with just my head projecting from the bivvy bag, I was content with the warm rain on my face, and the stream sliding gently past less than an arm's length away. The rain was of no concern. Almost soothing, it threatened no flooding, and I was sure it would be gone by daybreak. So I lay there rewinding our journey of the past five days, only vaguely anticipating days ahead and content with the now of being. Then, suddenly, my thoughts were interrupted— a frog had leapt from the water and landed on my forehead.

The rest of the night was spent with my head *inside* the bivvy bag.

MINT TEA WITH A MULETEER

Trekking with mules over a series of high passes, visiting Berber villages, and scrambling to unmarked summits had resulted in another memorable two-week journey in 1986. But at the end of the trek there was an alternative way out of the mountains that four of us wanted to take that would preclude the mules. Having no objections to our plan, the muleteers and the rest of our group agreed to meet us at the end of the day in a village close to the road-head, so we set out before dawn and clambered in the darkness aiming for a distant ridge . . . On this our last morning in the high mountains, my headtorch beam had lost much of its power, but day was now stealing into the sky and I could pick out a few recognisable features on the steep slope ahead. The other three were spread out—their flashes of white light growing dim, the sound of stones being rearranged by their boots, and the occasional voice caught in a fight for breath.

We came together to climb the gully. It was not a technical climb, rather a scramble over boulders, before we worked our way on ribs of rock, then steeply angled scree, followed by more rock ribs. Above these we stopped to rest, with legs dangling and eyes scanning peaks that emerged from anonymity with a blaze of red along their rim. Fifteen hundred feet below, I imagined I could see where we had spent the night.

It took two and a half hours to gain the ridge at the point we'd been aiming for, by which time day had fully formed. Gazing north we could now see far-off villages, but way beyond these, where mountains fell to the plains, a filter of haze blurred our vision. Lost in that haze Marrakech was no more than a memory and a name on a ticket home. Elsewhere, all was part of the vertical arena through which we'd traveled these past two weeks—a journey and a land we'd never forget. Strangers had become friends as we'd shared fresh experiences and daily excitements. And today would bring more.

On the other side of the ridge it was possible to traverse round the head of a hanging valley walled by north-facing crags, where we overlooked a wild inner sanctum of buttresses and pinnacles. Beneath our boots screes plunged into a gorge whose bed we could not see. It was the harshest of environments; a land without compromise; a take-it-or-leave-it land. We took it at face value and launched ourselves down the screes into the unknown, filling our boots with grit and leaving in our wake clouds of dust.

At the foot of the screes a new valley system opened up, the couloirs that sliced its massive gray walls clogged still with last winter's snow, while we fought our way through a leveling of boulders and waist-high patches of thistle. Cascades poured over a bluff as the valley enticed us forward, dropping from one level to the next, growing more colorful the deeper it led.

Now we had a stream for company, its water eager to reach the plains, surging forward towards the north, tumbling over projections as it went, swirling along pebble corridors—the perfect companion on such a day. Where it dashed against rocks, tiny rainbows appeared in the spray; then it was drawn into the narrows of a gorge and the rainbows were lost in shadow. Descent here was difficult at first, but the way soon eased, so we could walk rather than scramble and pause to inspect and admire cushion plants clinging to the gorge walls, where they'd been dampened by a waterfall spilling over the topmost cliffs. As we gazed up at the spray individual droplets became diamonds suspended in sunlight. At the base of the falls, a deep green pool had formed. Resisting the temptation to bathe, we satisfied ourselves with dunking heads and letting the water run down our sweat- and dust-stained bodies.

Half an hour later a mule was seen drinking from the stream, and in the shade of an overhanging boulder nearby a fresh-faced Berber was tending a fire. The smell of juniper rose in the smoke to mingle with that of mint and mule dung.

The man was not alone, for a woman appeared from the other side of the boulder clutching a handful of freshly picked mint, a round-faced infant tucked under one arm. Dressed in a symphony of reds and greens, she washed the leaves, shook them over the stream, then pushed them into a pot with delicate fingers. And a shy smile spread across her face when her husband asked if we wanted tea. So we sat with them in the shade, drank mint tea with the muleteer, and watched as swifts dashed to and fro in a feeding frenzy, their nests plastered to the great walls soaring above us.

Sipping my third glass of the hot sweet liquid, I was reminded that days in the mountains are more than just mountains, and the Atlas experience has many dimensions. And that is just how it should be. Not just in the Atlas, but everywhere.

PYRENEES

A Spiritual Home

E ntering Spain on the way to Morocco in 1965, our truck crossed
the Basque country as daybreak stole from the sky, with the Pyrenees depicted in that soft light as little more than low misted hills.
Weeks later, with Atlas dust grimed into our clothes, we returned via
the eastern end of the range, with heavy rain obscuring any view
of the mountains. The High Pyrenees would have to wait. And then
when I did get to see them at last, it was only as a distant outline
from the swift-nested ramparts of Carcasonne—a ragged horizon
turning purple when the sun dropped. Having run out of money I
turned to hitch my way home.

But the Pyrenees were worth waiting for. A first visit revealed
snow-capped 10,000 foot peaks, modest glaciers, fragrant valleys
and canyons, hundreds of sparkling lakes and the richest mountain
flora in all Europe. I'd have to return. So I did. Again and again, year
after year, until the Pyrenees became my spiritual home.

To help pay for mountain holidays, I was writing magazine features about the Pyrenees at a time when no-one else was doing so. One day I received a call from Walt Unsworth, editor at the time of *Climber and Rambler,* one of only two or three outdoors magazines on the market in the UK. He'd started a small guidebook-publishing business. Would I be interested in writing a guide to the Pyrenees? Having never looked at a guidebook before, let alone used one, I did some basic research to find out what sort of information was required for such a book. It seemed straightforward enough, and the prospect of becoming a published author did wonders for my ego. So I signed the contract and set to.

First published in 1978, *Walks and Climbs in the Pyrenees* is still in print, providing an endless set of excuses to revisit those enchanted mountains to walk, trek and climb as I gather material for new editions and updated reprints. And every visit is cause for celebration.

OUT OF THE SHADOWS INTO THE LIGHT

Previous visits had given a hint that the Pyrenees needed further examination, and I was eager to explore. Money was in short supply, and time had to be carefully balanced; my work as a youth hostel warden precluded any leave in the prime climbing season, so we went when we could and hoped for the best. At home in the early summer of 1973 wild flowers patterned the meadows, but in the Pyrenees winter had not yet run its course.

It had been a long and heavy winter in the mountains, and the beginning of June was too early to be there. Snow still lay deep at low altitudes, while avalanches peeled from slopes exposed to the sun. Keith Sweeting and I were both nervous, but tried to hide those nerves as we ploughed our way up long tongues of stone-pocked snow. Burdened by over-heavy rucksacks, every few paces one or the other would break through the crust to wallow in the soft underlay or find boots submerged in a hidden stream. As a consequence our feet were soaked, our legs cold, our lungs raw from exertion. We were not fit.

It was late afternoon before we found the hut. Half-buried by avalanche debris, it took almost an hour to dig our way to the door and force entry. It was like an igloo inside. Snow had come down the chimney and spread across the stone floor, and although it only took four paces to cross the room, each step was deadly. Our shelter was an ice rink. One and a half candles, a damp box of matches, an empty wine bottle, and a half packet of rice lay on a shelf beside the chimney breast; there were no mattresses on the bare boards of the two sleeping platforms, but it would be our home for the night.

We cooked and ate outside, sitting on the roof gazing up at the frontier ridge, at scars in the snow where rocks and other debris had scraped evil-looking runnels, wondering how safe it would be to cross that final slope in the morning. It looked prime avalanche terrain, but if we set out early it should be okay. Less than an hour, surely, and we would be on safe ground. "Easy," said Keith. "It'll be a doddle."

In the night came a muffled "whoompf" and the door shook. I turned over and went back to sleep, but in the morning we had to climb out of the window as another avalanche (a small one, thankfully) had targeted the hut and blocked the door.

If we could, we would have tiptoed up and across the final snow slope that led to the Port de Venasque, but when you're wearing big boots and have everything you'll need for two weeks in the mountains on your back—two weeks' worth of food, fuel for the cooker, climbing gear, and tent—tiptoeing is not an option. But we trod as lightly as we could and kept a decent space between us, hearts racing, ears alert for the slightest hint that the slope was about to go. Despite the chill, sweat formed on my brow. My toes and fingers were frozen, but my palms were moist. Keith was uncharacteristically silent.

Deep in shadow I aimed for a narrow V of light that gave the only hint of where the pass should be. I'd read about that slim breach in the rocks, a classic crossing place from France to Spain where the winds howl and neither father waits for son nor son for father. Now we were about to cross it ourselves—if the slope would allow, that is. Each step gave a heartening crunch, but my boots barely dented the surface. Overhead rocks were glazed with ice. It could have been January instead of June, but my confidence grew.

Then the pass was revealed as a shimmer of sunlight glanced across crags that formed its western wall. The slope steepened, I kicked the toes of my boots into the crust, leaned on my axe, and heaved myself out of the shadows of France and into the sunlight of Spain. From darkness into light; from winter into summer.

Across the head of the Ésera valley, the Maladeta massif bared its glaciers and snowfields, above one of which rose the pristine Pico de Aneto, highest of all Pyrenean summits. For this very moment I had dreamed all winter long.

At last! The Promised Land.

UP AND OVER

At over 11,168ft, Pico de Aneto ("Nethou" to the French) has the highest summit in the Pyrenees. First climbed in 1842, the standard route takes about five hours or so from the Renclusa refugio via the Aneto glacier, which these days is shrinking fast. In June 1973 it was somewhat different when we made a north to south traverse of the mountain. It's just one of a number of ascents I've made in the Maladeta massif over the years, but it remains one of the most memorable.

Dawn broke as we topped the ridge separating the Maladeta's glacier from that of Aneto, giving the perfect excuse to pause for a moment, to settle our breathing and watch as the sun climbed out of a distant hollow to cast its light on mountains filling every horizon. To the east the Forcanada shrugged its way out of a sea of cloud, and beyond that double-pronged peak one summit after another paid homage to the new day.

On the ridge wind-scuffed snow made for a cautious walk along the crest, where we skirted the insignificant Pico del Portillon Superior to reach the gap of the *portillon* itself. Peering into the gully that would lead onto the glacier, we discussed the need for crampons, but gambled on our ability to deal with the hard-packed snow-ice without them.

All the way from the foot of the gully to Aneto's summit appeared to be an unmarked snowfield masking a glacier; and beyond a mound, which we took to be a pile of rocks, our ascent would take a direct route to the top of that graceful cone on a vast sheet of untrod powder whose pristine qualities both invited and excited us.

What's more, we had the world to ourselves, for we'd seen no-one since arriving in the valley five days ago. The Renclusa *refugio* was still locked and shuttered, and the squalid annex next door had received no visitors for weeks. It was too late for ski touring; too early for walkers and climbers. Unaware of our good fortune we'd arrived in a period of transition; we had winter's purity above 5,000 feet, but the first flowers bursting into life below the snow-line where we'd left the tent. Summer was still some way off. Now on Aneto's snow-covered glacier we had perfect conditions—and not a single boot print to follow.

As we prodded for unseen crevasses, the only sounds to disturb the morning were the squeak and scrunch of boots on the frozen crust—and our breathing. Despite the rising sun our breath steamed, but by the time we were halfway across the glacier the temperature was soaring and the soles of our boots balled with softening snow. The rhythm of ascent was interrupted now by the need to tap those balls free with our axes.

Above the Collado de Coronas the narrow ridge of the Pont de Mahomet brought us back to reality, for here the rocks were glazed with a winter's worth of hard ice, and we were glad of the rope. Minutes later, and five hours after leaving the tent, I stood beside the summit cross and took a long, much-needed drink from my water bottle. Keith handed over some chocolate, and only then did we examine the vast array of peak, ridge, and valley that fell away in every direction. So much was new to us; so many peaks unknown, untrod; so many valleys containing secrets. I felt a buzz of excitement in the sheer mystery of the world laid bare before us. On Aneto's summit dreams were born, ambitions took shape. The Pyrenees, surely, would supply all the outdoor adventure a man could need, and I was ready for it.

Dragging myself out of dreams, I was aware that the sky was changing, so with our plan to make a north–south traverse of Aneto still intact, we studied our downward route on the south side of the mountain, comparing reality with its depiction on our map, and prepared to leave.

Retracing our route across the Pont de Mahomet to the Collado de Coronas, we then cut down to the left onto a little glacier tilting steeply into a basin. According to the map there were tarns down there, but as everything was plastered with snow we could only guess where they might be and trust that, should we wander across them, their covering of ice would be strong enough to support our weight. Taking a cold bath was not on our list of things to do that day.

Down we went, with an occasional involuntary glissade, losing height quickly until the gradient eased. There we unroped, stashed the rope on top of my rucksack and, looking back up the slope towards the summit cliffs (so different this side of the mountain), we noticed that the sky had disappeared and a gray wash of mist was spilling over the ridge. Morning's promise had run out.

But we were past caring now. As the snow softened, thinned and turned to mush on our continued descent, we knew the day was ours. There were more ice-coated tarns, easy to avoid with water showing round their edges; there were streams and marshy areas; soldanellas—those tiny, tassle-headed harbingers of spring—poked through spatters of old snow. There was avalanche debris, a few spindly trees, then woods of pine and fir, and as the first crack of thunder sounded and rain began, we spied a glass-fronted hut and made a beeline for it.

Our timing, for once, had been impeccable.

THE LAST GREEN VALLEY

In the central High Pyrenees the Ésera valley had a rare perfection that called me back many times. By going early in the season we had both the mountains and the valley to ourselves; there was an air of untouched purity that was too good to last. But in the late summer of 1975 reality had invaded . . .

Snow lay most of the way down into the valley, becoming soft, shallow, and patchy as we lost height. Where it was melting, tan-colored grass was speckled with tiny soldanellas. Streams gurgled and a breeze carried the sound of a cascade we could not see. Below the last patch of snow two fat salamanders waddled across our path as though on sore feet, their vivid orange and black markings defying any attempt at camouflage.

We found a terrace of dry ground on which our tent would not only give a view of the Maladeta but would enable us to see down-valley to the peaks of Literole. Behind it ran a clear stream, in the midst of which lay a flat rock on which I would sit and dream or draw water for cooking. From the tent a small defile focused attention onto a lower terrace where, that very first day, I watched an izard (the Pyrenean chamois) drinking from the same stream—our stream.

Within moments of our arrival Keith had gone hunting for pine tufts. A stand of low-growing conifers stood a short distance from our terrace; there was also a riot of juniper that smelled sweetly when crushed, and clumps of alpenrose waiting to erupt into bloom. But it was pine he was after. He returned with an armful of tufts taken from winter-damaged trees; these he spread on the ground before pitching the tent over them, so when we settled to sleep at night we had a soft mattress beneath the groundsheet, and the fragrance of pine was disturbed each time one of us turned over.

When mosquitoes visited at dusk, he'd erect a tripod of tent pegs at the open door. From the tripod he suspended another tuft, under which he lit a stub of candle; not too close, but near enough to singe it, sending a wisp of smoke rising in the doorway to keep the mozzies at bay, and at the same time adding to the fresh smell of pine inside the tent.

For two weeks we had the valley to ourselves. Not just the valley, but the mountains that walled it. We'd climb all day and see no-one, returning late in the afternoon to discover new flowers emerging from the grass around the tent; there were trumpet gentians, primulas, two types of orchid, and a scattering of dog's tooth violets. We'd walk for hours through open meadows of flowers; the tiniest of blue butterflies would drift around us; we'd hear marmots calling fresh from hibernation, and watch as a small herd of izard loped across a snowslip. Alpenrose buds now opened, and our tent was surrounded by color. The valley became a valley of flowers, a valley of rare perfection. And for two unforgettable weeks it was our own private playground.

We got to know the mountains through personal discovery. The only English-language guidebook had been published in 1862, so we made our own way and our own mistakes. If we reached the summit we aimed for, we'd celebrate. If we failed, well . . . if we'd had a good day we'd celebrate anyway. There was no-one to impress or condemn us; there were no paths, no cairns, no signposts. Nature had full dominion.

Day by day the valley was being transformed by nature. On one occasion we set out to climb a peak on the frontier ridge. Just below its crags we came upon a pool in a scoop of grass, rock, and snow. Around its edge tadpoles twitched, but the water was clear enough to turn distant mountains on their heads. When we'd descended into the valley a few days earlier it must have been hidden beneath a cover of ice and snow, and we would have walked straight across it. But when we came back this way at the end of our fortnight's tenancy the pool had disappeared, leaving just a black tidemark. In those two weeks the valley had gone from winter through spring and into full summer.

There was no forgetting such a valley. At home I'd wake at night and immediately be transported there; I'd smell the pine and the flowers and imagine the orange glow of daybreak spreading across the mountains. So next year we were back, and nothing had changed. We went at the same time and again saw no-one. It was just the two of us, with the marmots and flowers and the occasional stray izard drinking from our stream. Or us drinking from his. We made new climbs and repeated others we'd enjoyed the year before, and every day was special.

But the magic was destined not to last. We tried again the following June, but failed to make it over the mountains, kept at bay by an endless succession of storm and avalanche. So I went back in September, when success would be guaranteed—this time with my wife and daughters, for I longed to share with them the secrets of this valley of flowers.

We made a devious approach. Not for us a direct crossing of the frontier ridge; we would come to the valley by stealth, through Spain. So we took our time, drifted from valley to valley, checking out massifs to climb and explore in the years ahead, savoring countless pleasures of the High Pyrenees, gradually working our way closer, drawn by memories and a deeply satisfying air of anticipation.

There was a road pushing north from Benasque. It had been there many years before on my first ever visit to these mountains, but it didn't go far—only to the dammed lake and no farther. A track replaced the road and led us northward.

In 1897 Harold Spender came down the valley of the Ésera from its source among the glaciers. In his account of the journey he mentioned this track: "We passed the baths of Venasque . . . and a little below came across some Spanish workmen employed on a road in a desultory fashion. Whether that road will ever be finished is a matter that must rest on the knees of the gods."

Now, as we came to the Baños de Benasque—Spender's baths of Venasque—I saw that the gods had made their decision. Below, on the broad river plain, a contractor's vehicle belched clouds of diesel smoke.

Dusk was drawing in by the time we turned the bend into the upper sanctuary, and we were still on the bulldozed track that had not been there 18 months before. It led deeper into the valley with an urgency I feared. A concrete ford had been created through the river, and where vehicles had used it their skidding tyres had ripped the vegetation on both banks. A once-sacred meadowland was scarred with dried mud and the imprints of wheels, not animals. Dwarf rhododendrons had been desecrated, and rainbow swirls of oil colored puddles in the track.

A sense of foreboding hung over me, and with every step I slipped deeper into a pool of dejection.

One hundred and fifty feet from the site of the idyllic terrace on which Keith and I had camped, the rough track finally came to a halt. Three cars were parked there; two Spanish, one French. Cardboard boxes lay strewn among the shrubbery, rotting after a shower of rain. Wine bottles had been smashed against a rock. Toilet paper fluttered from the branches of a pine tree, and tin cans were rusting in the stream.

"Urban motorised man," wrote Fernando Barrientos Fernandez, "has no responsible conservationist regard for nature."

I walked sadly up to that special terrace to discover a metal workman's hut positioned exactly where we'd had our tent in those cherished times of mountain beauty. Innocent days, they were. But now the site was desecrated, the valley's innocence betrayed.

It was too late to think of leaving, so we pitched our tent without enthusiasm as darkness swallowed the ugly intrusions. Up on the Maladeta's slopes a shepherd's campfire glowed like a beacon. The glaciers were barely perceived, yet a shadowy profile against distant snows announced that the mountains still remained. But in the night I awoke from a disturbed sleep as a wind came from the west. It found a sheet of polythene and sent it flapping against the tent's guys.

"Where," I wondered, "will the izard go to drink now?"

....

A version of this story appeared in *The Great Outdoors* for September 1978 and was subsequently reprinted in the 1981 anthology *The Winding Trail*, published by Diadem.

⌃

IT WAS THE NIGHTINGALE

In the summer of 2000 I was alone in the mountains, drifting from France to Spain and back again—climbing, walking, checking routes for a new edition of my guidebook. In high places there would be the croaking of choughs, a tuneless sound that was nonetheless an integral part of the mountain scene. Yet one evening, down in a valley, a much sweeter sound romanced my senses . . . Driven from the mountains by a storm that washed the hills and threatened to drown valleys I came to an empty campsite below a plug of rock, upon which was crouched a tiny, cracked Spanish village—a dozen houses crowded among cobbled alleys, a church, and a view of the High Pyrenees brooding under an evil sky. Although the storm rattled as I pitched my tent, the site was safe from flooding. The rain eased while I cooked and ate my meal, and only a light drizzle was spattering the flysheet when I drifted into sleep.

Suddenly I awoke to a sound made in heaven. Behind the tent a nightingale warbled and trilled its liquid song; a song that had no end, no sign of ending, it rose and fell and rose again and again, tossing notes to unseen stars as the hours moved toward midnight and beyond. I crawled out in a vain attempt to see the source, but all was dark save for the distant flash of lightning behind black, shapeless mountains. The nightingale cared nothing for that far-off storm, but sang as though all of life depended on it.

Next day the storm was forgotten, and the sun scorched a cloudless sky as I scrambled past waterfalls born of yesterday's deluge and looked on peaks dusted with overnight snow that would melt by midday. Then, as evening drew in, I was seduced back to the nightingale camp and stretched out on the grass beside my tent as darkness fell. It was then that the nightingale returned and in an instant his melodies rippled through the valley.

Hour upon hour I lay, reluctant to sleep. The moon-free night was filled with beauty, and shortly after midnight the solo became a duet as a second nightingale copied the song from a tree across the way—note for note, phrase for phrase it echoed the melody in perfect pitch. Nightingales in stereo, sufficient to melt the coldest heart, the birds were romancing one another, and their love duet filled the night with what seemed like audible honey.

Eventually I drifted into a light sleep. When I woke again around 4am they were still at it! But now they were growing weary, the pause between each new melody a little more prolonged than the last. Yet still they sang until the very first stain of sunrise stretched across the eastern hills. Only then did the birds give their throats a rest. And I . . . well, I gave up on sleep and headed for the mountains once more.

▲

TRAGEDY ON JEAN-PIERRE

Mike and I were brought up in neighboring villages, started climbing together in north Wales, and several years later shared a rope in the Atlas Mountains. He had a natural talent on rock, and for a while we planned to open a climbing school in Snowdonia, but our lives took different directions and inevitably that dream faded. However, in 1977 the opportunity came to share a rope once more, so we headed for the Pyrenees with an ambitious list of routes, but from Day One things did not go according to plan.

Afternoon was well advanced when we arrived at the foot of Pic du Midi's south-facing Pombie Wall, and by the time we'd pitched the tent shadows were marching across the face. At the same time the valley below was filling with cloud, and its tide was creeping up the hillside too, engulfing all in its path. Yet there were still climbers at work up there; about halfway to the top by the sound of it. We could hear their voices, the clatter of hardware, the ring of a peg being hammered into a crack. No doubt they would be facing a bivvy tonight.

Too late in the day to attempt anything ourselves, and before even making a brew, we were drawn towards the mountain while we could still see it, and we'd just reached the screes when the sound all climbers dread came to us.

Stonefall. A lot of it.

We looked up to see a stream of dust and a fusillade of rocks bouncing down the face. Large rocks, small rocks, and a shower of stones began high up, then gathered momentum as they spun into open space. We automatically flinched and stopped in our tracks to see where they'd land, and it didn't take much imagination to know that if any climbers were near that lot, they'd be dry-mouthed with fear.

In moments the face was swallowed by cloud, and as individual features disappeared the frantic crash of rock against rock gradually lessened and finally ended, followed by an eerie silence. Then the silence was broken by a concerned voice calling: "Henri."

Silence.

Again, but more urgently this time: "Henri!"

Then louder still: "HENRI!"

There was desperation in that cry, but it was nothing compared with the sound that followed. A sound that broke your heart. From that sound a single word tore free from a mangled expression of grief. A single word one did not need to be a linguist to understand.

"Mort!"

Mike and I faced one another, eyes wide with horror.

The clouds that enveloped Pic du Midi brought early nightfall, and the rescue team arrived as the last vestige of light was disappearing. The helicopter could first be heard in the distance, then it was overhead, where it hovered only about a 300 feet above us, searching the gloom for what seemed an eternity before it began to descend. In poor visibility there was no room for error, but the pilot knew what he was doing and set the chopper down close to the Pombie refuge, whose guardian had alerted the *gendarmerie* when I'd run in with the news, leaving Mike to try to make contact with the survivor. The chopper blades slowed, then ceased moving.

My ears stopped ringing, and the guardian's voice dropped to a normal volume.

An air of calm emanated from the team; they were professional, unflustered, deliberate in their movements. Each one knew his role, so three helmeted climbers roped up, switched on headtorches, and with a final word of instruction from their leader, set off in the now damp, cloud-wrapped darkness towards the unseen mountain—the mountain affectionately known to local climbers as Jean-Pierre. A walkie-talkie crackled. Someone lit a cigarette; its glow penetrated the gloom.

As the minutes ticked by disembodied voices could be heard—one at the foot of the mountain; the other high, distant and trembling. There would be long periods when only one voice could be heard; the higher of the two. But when the other answered it always came from a different position, marked sometimes by a brief flash of light when the mist allowed. Seemingly undeterred by either darkness or fog, the rescue team was making steady progress up the Pombie Wall. Mike and I were mere spectators while a drama played out above us. Chastened, we returned to our tent.

Later that night the rescue team located and secured the body, then climbed up to the survivor and sat with him through the dark, empty hours. In the safe comfort of our tent, I too was unable to sleep and maintained a silent vigil with them.

The new day dawned with Jean-Pierre cloud-free. The helicopter took off, swept across the face of the mountain, hovered there for a while, then rose to land on the flat summit, where two of the rescue team and the survivor were waiting. The third team member was later lifted from the face along with the rockfall victim, the two seen swinging free at the end of a long cable.

The victim and survivor had our sympathy; the rescue team our respect. But for Mike and me Pic du Midi's Pombie Wall had lost its appeal. We'd climb something else.

THE LONGEST DAY

When summer climbs are dreamed of at home during the winter months, ideas and ambitions often outstrip reality. Sometimes the weather gods conspire against the best-laid plans, and time runs out before much can be achieved, as Keith and I found in the late spring of 1975.

The shepherd's hut was as squalid inside as it had first appeared from across the stream when we'd spied it through the storm. About three paces long by two wide, it had a low, absorbent roof through which the rain dripped at unsuitably strategic points. A makeshift shutter was placed against a tiny window, and when it was removed the squall burst in. There was only a broken pane of glass in this window. The floor was the same granite as the mountains that rose on three sides, as uneven as a sheet of corrugated iron and littered with the droppings of innumerable sheep. Cows had been outside; sheep inside. Fortunately there were neither this morning, and the hut was deserted. It was also cold, damp, and smelly. Against one wall leaned a rough bench, and the only remaining item of furniture was a shelf suspended on wire hooks from the ceiling.

It wasn't much, but with every crash of thunder we were thankful for its existence. This was no day to be caught crossing a high pass, which had been our plan when we'd struck camp a couple of hours earlier.

Our first task now was to get out of wet clothes and find the means by which to hang them. Drying facilities were negligible, but at least there was room for the rain gear to drip while we enjoyed the luxury of shirt and trousers that were not soaked through.

Outside the storm continued its attack with sheets of rain and a wind that rattled both the door and the temporary shutter at the window. It was a vicious morning that bore no resemblance to the dreams that had sustained me all winter long, and had brought us here with summer optimism and an ambitious list of routes to climb and passes to cross. This storm had a permanent feel to it. It would not blow itself out in an hour or two. It would not flee to other mountains, other valleys. It was trapped here, as we were, by a semi-circle of peaks that turned our cirque into a turbulent cauldron.

Keith settled himself on the bench and rolled a cigarette, and when that was finished he suggested we light a fire. "Go and find some decent wood," he said, "while I start things off with this little heap of kindling." He motioned to a small pile of sticks laced with cobwebs beside the fireplace.

I glared at him, hating the way he'd contrived to stay inside while I braved the storm once more, but said nothing. Pulling on my cold, wet, so-called rain gear, I went outside and slithered down to the stream beside which I remembered seeing some dead wood. Moss coated and mud-spattered it was not the most satisfactory fuel, but the long-dead branches would have to do. My search for better firewood would not lead far in this weather.

Twenty minutes later the hut was filled with smoke that burned our eyes and started uncontrollable bouts of coughing. I fled outside, clambered onto the roof, and removed the stone slab that covered the chimney. With that the smoke billowed into my face.

"Thanks," said Keith. "That's a great improvement."

Seconds tediously multiplied into minutes, and the minutes slowly drifted into hours. The fire flared and settled; it crackled and spat. Occasionally a downdraft blew smoke into the room. Sheep dung was fed onto the slow-burning wood, and our clothing took on its odour. Outside the storm showed no sign of easing.

Morning reached maturity, became mid-day. We would eat.

Keith was fastidious over the preparation of a weak soup, but it was I who had to brave the tumult for water.

All the food we'd brought from home to last a fortnight in the hills was carefully set out. This was food to sustain long days—not in crude shepherd's huts, but on sunlit climbs from a camp in the valley beyond the mountains, now barred to us by lightning. At home every item had been calculated by weight rather than proper nutritional value; there was little to spare, and like politicians balancing the budget we estimated days remaining, meals required, and the demands for brews. There were no excesses, no allowances for days like this, when even the simple task of making an extra tea or coffee could be justified as a means of combating boredom to help survive this unexpected, unwelcome, and endless day.

In the middle of the afternoon the storm drew breath, allowing the sun to make a feeble appearance through layers of cloud, taunting us with a glimpse of rock walls spattered with new snow, and when I stepped outside and turned to the west I convinced myself that I could almost see the pass that would enable our escape. But not today, for the storm returned once more as the only certainty in these uncertain times. Fine-weather climbs, I decided, live only in memory and anticipation of a bright future. The present was no more than a revolving carousel of thunder, lightning, and torrential rain.

An hour later the fury built to Wagnerian proportions; our poor leaking shelter stood in the vortex and would have shaken to its very foundations, if it had foundations, which it hadn't. Instead, it appeared to rock with every thunderous eruption. Glistening lines of water ran down the walls to form rivulets on the floor; the ceiling dripped and our misery increased. And it was then that we received a visitor.

Out of the smoke, down the soot-blackened chimney, emerged a rat. With sorrowful eyes that pierced the gloom it pleaded for mercy. The hell in here, it seemed to say, is nothing compared with the hell outside. Then it made a traverse of the end wall, negotiated an overhang, and shrank into a tiny crack that could be used for a bivouac. And there it remained for the rest of the day, untroubled and untroubling, invisible save for a pair of sad eyes and a damp nose.

I knew exactly how it felt.

Day was almost over and we had achieved nothing. In the world beyond the storm perhaps the sun was descending to a far-off valley. In our hut it had never been anything brighter than twilight all day, and now the air was growing much, much colder. Perhaps it would snow overnight. I looked at my watch and announced it was time to eat. We'd prepare a decent meal this time, subdue our despair with something tasty—something that didn't have the flavor of monosodium glutamate. But in the middle of our fantasising, Keith suddenly said: "Hey, have you considered where we'll sleep?"

"No."

Neither of us had given a thought to night's approach, being fixated by the storm and dreams of food beyond our reach. And a forlorn hope of escape. But as I looked around me, at pools of tan-colored water and boot-flattened sheep dung, I knew this stinking hut would not do for a bedroom.

"You'll just have to face the weather after all," I told him, and suddenly felt much brighter. "You'll have to go outside and put the tent up before darkness falls."

"Me? Why me?"

"It's your tent."

So he went outside while I took his place beside the fire and began to prepare our meal. And I smiled for the first time that day as I listened to the rain smacking against the hut and the symphony of the storm outside. If anything, it was growing wilder out there, and he was gone a long, long time.

Then the door burst open and he was silhouetted in its opening. Water poured from his clothes; his long hair was matted and rain dripped from his nose.

"What d'you want first?" he asked. "The good news or the bad news?"

My heart sank. "Let's have the bad news first."

"Well," he began, "there's only one possible place for the tent. And that's on a load of cowshit."

"And the good news?"

"It's still warm!"

C'EST LE PARADIS

In 2007 another solo trip to the Pyrenees to research routes for the guidebook gave an excuse to explore one or two areas I'd not visited before. Being alone is a luxury, for you can indulge yourself in long days of activity or hours of reverie without the need to consider anyone else. If you set your own agenda, but keep your options open, it's interesting to see how each day unfolds.

Spain was well into summer, but on the other side of the mountain, in the remote Ariège region of France, a memory of winter lingered, with snow banked high on the hillsides and ice floes in the lakes. After a long morning's approach I'd spent an hour dreaming by one such lake, its depths confused by layers of old ice still clinging to the shoreline, where spring was a reluctant visitor. Then I descended for ten minutes to discover a cascade erupting from a cleft of rock, draining the lake and crashing 65 feet below in a turmoil of spray. An exposed mattress of heather was too tempting to ignore, so I gave in and sprawled there, just out of range, to capture the essence of the scene—the fury of sound, the constant beat of water on rock, rainbows tossed like a bride's bouquet into the air.

Later I dragged myself away and wound down the mountain for 650 feet or more among dwarf pine and juniper into a glacial basin glistening with streams and pools, where spring had arrived with its bounty of goodness, vitality, and promise. Water ran everywhere, and when the path disappeared a line of cairns, created in a drier season than this, directed a way across and mocked any attempt to retain dry feet. But wet feet didn't matter, for such was the beauty of that basin that every sense was enticed into activity. Tiny islands of granite emerged from the water. Domes of grass, alpenrose, and bilberry created archipelagos of color. Meadowlands 6 feet wide were covered in gentian, spring anemone, soldanella, and sweet-smelling daphne, while marsh marigolds bobbed their gold medallion heads along the edge of every rushing stream. Birds flitted from rock to rock, marmots whistled, and the distant boom of cascades echoed throughout the valley.

Perched upon a rock amidst all this water, absorbing the miracle of rebirth and bewitched by the abundant goodness all around me, I knew yet again the gift of sheer happiness. There was nowhere else I'd rather be. Life's cup was full and overflowing.

Then my solitude was disturbed by a neatly dressed couple (they had to be French) making a beeline towards me, splashing calf-deep through the streams without concern. Stopping a few paces away the man spread his arms wide and, with eyes blazing, gasped: "C'est le paradis!"

And I couldn't argue with that.

· · ·

A PYRENEAN MAESTRO

After spending days climbing routes on Pic du Midi in the late summer of 1984, Alan Payne and I moved on to the granite peaks of the Balaïtous massif that loomed to the east. Bold, solid-looking mountains that carry the Franco-Spanish border, they dominate a wild, lake-spattered landscape around which a few simple huts are located.

We caught sight of Refuge d'Arrémoulit as we edged along the narrow and exposed Passage d'Orteig 650 feet above Lac d'Artouste. A tiny blob of roofed stone, it was dwarfed by slabs and boulders that lay among tarns at the foot of Pic Palas. From a distance it appeared deserted, and when we eventually arrived at the door our initial suspicion proved correct; the hut was deserted—apart, that is, from the guardian, who appeared from the shadows rubbing his eyes with no attempt to hide the fact that he'd just fallen out of bed. It was mid-afternoon, and Alan and I had been on the go for six hours.

"Bonjour," yawned the guardian. "You look hot."

It *was* hot, and heat from the early September sun bounced off the smooth granite to emphasize the fact.

"Any chance of a beer?"

"It's in the fridge," said the guardian, and led us round the back of the hut where several bottles were submerged in a spring-fed pool. He handed one to Alan, another to me, and took one for himself, then pulled a penknife from his pocket and yanked the top from each one.

Never did beer taste so good.

Rucksacks slid from our backs to lean against the wall, and with sweat-stained shirts draped over rocks we lowered ourselves to the ground to relax against the front of the building—with a second bottle waiting to be drained clutched in our hands or held against a burning brow. I'd drink this one slowly, to allow the flavor to settle.

After a few short, monosyllabic questions about where we'd come from and were we planning to stay the night, the guardian fell silent and let the afternoon's peace settle around us.

Trapped in a landscape of stone and still water there were practically no sounds. No birds sang. No streams gurgled. No stones clattered into a far-off gully. If it had not been for the blood coursing through my veins, the only certainty that I'd not grown deaf was the distant thrum that spoke of the Earth spinning in space.

After some time a shadow moved across my face. Opening one eye I saw the guardian slip quietly into the hut and was vaguely aware of his bare feet padding on the stone floor. Moments later he reappeared, carrying a flute in his right hand, its silver dazzling in the sunshine. Choosing a rocky perch above the nearest small lake twenty paces from Alan and me, he settled cross-legged, like a bearded maestro facing an audience full of expectation. I nudged Alan, and when he opened his eyes I nodded towards the flautist, who now had our undivided attention.

This would be good—imagine! Big bold mountains reflecting the sun, an azure lake, a mind at peace fully receptive to the subtleties of some lyrical composition. The acoustics would be interesting here at 7,500 feet; the music would echo across the lake to produce a delayed stereo effect. It would be a unique experience; one to savor. A solitary flute to serenade and soften a harsh wilderness. Mozart, perhaps? Or something modern?

I took another sip of beer, leaned back against the hut's wall and closed my eyes again. Then held my breath as I pictured the guardian raising the instrument to his face, one elbow at right angles to his body. he'd moisten his lips with his tongue, then launch into his repertoire.

But the peace of the mountains was rudely shattered—and with it our anticipation—as the guardian, a musical novice, practiced his scales. Over and over and over again.

The flute screeched, and badly constructed notes spattered on warm granite slabs and scratched at our ears. It was an insult both to music and to the natural harmonies of the landscape. So we drained our beer and scampered to some far corner of the mountains where the scrooping could not be heard. And silence returned.

We understood, then, why the hut was empty.

SOMETHING OF A DOO-DAY

Even as far south as the Pyrenees it's possible to experience a snowstorm in the middle of summer, although it's pretty rare. A "normal" summer in those mountains will give wall-to-wall blue skies and blazing sunshine day after day, broken now and then by a sudden violent storm which clears the air. My climbing trip in 1985 saw days of oppressive heat that doubled the effort of every upward movement, and I longed for a cloud with the promise of rain or even snow. But none came.

A couple of hours above Lac d'Oô and its famed waterfall, we left our overnight camp and laboured up the trail on yet another cloud-free morning. A hazy blue tarpaulin of sky stretched between peaks that towered on either side, trapping yesterday's air. In an hour's time the sun would heat the old paved slabs of the trail to egg-frying temperatures, so we were eager to make height in the hope of a breeze before that happened. But we were weary, and height was hard to gain and slow to win.

Deserting the paved way that leads to the Refuge du Portillon, a faint trail of cairns took us steeply up a series of rough slopes beside cliffs and slabs and over boggy patches in which we left two sets of black bootprints betraying our passage across. Then the sun shot over the mountains and poured both light and heat into our basin, leaving us with nowhere to hide. Off to our left the big morning-black walls of Pics Quayrat and Lézat teased us with shade, but sadly our route was not that way. There would be no shade where we were going. Above our right shoulders crags that linked Pic des Spijeoles with Pic Gourdon reflected the sun and taunted our frailties as we stumbled over a rock barrier to catch a first sighting of Lac Glacé. It looked tempting, but was too far below to even consider a dip.

In 1787 Ramond de Carbonnières discovered this deep green pool, which was then completely frozen below three glaciers. But on this morning of thrumming heat, Lac Glacé bore a tiny flotilla of icebergs, and only a shallow, pink-stained remnant of glacier lay draped across the upper wilderness of stone that supported the frontier ridge. Ramond thought it "the most beautiful desert of the kind [he] had seen in the Pyrenees." But knowing that our route led up that wilderness challenged my perception of beauty, and nothing on our way to the frontier ridge made me change my mind. In that heat it was grim, bare, and forbidding.

A short descent was followed by a haul up a band of rocks, over scree and across a boulderland before another misery of steep, unstable scree that shifted with every step. It was a nightmare of a treadmill, aggravated by dust that rose with every slip and slither. Up a step, down a slide, then up again. One more step, then another; a stumble, a slide, a step, and a grunt of effort. Suddenly Alan started an avalanche of stones and swept past me. The whole slope began to move; acres of scree gathered pace and slid towards the lake, and we with it. I lunged in desperation and grabbed a firm piece of Pic Jean Arlaud, which arrested my slide.

Alan did likewise, and we clung on as the scree continued down without us.

Port d'Oô brought relief. Until we studied the route down, that is. Sitting astride the ridge at a little under 10,000 feet, our descent to the south looked as bad as our ascent had been, but across the hidden depths of the Estós valley rose our old friend, Pico de Posets. Bold of outline, but broken and unstable close at hand, today it was daubed with less snow than I'd ever known it. Despite that it beckoned as of old, and in a day or two we'd renew our acquaintance. But first we had to descend into Spain, and the temperature was rising.

Terraces of scree-covered rock led down to a minefield of boulders, between which we were forced to thread our way, balancing over and between them; it was furnace-like, no air could circulate, and we baked, sweated, and gasped. As I leaped from one to another, or stepped gingerly onto a slab that rocked, my legs turned to jelly. Then I missed my footing and dropped between a couple of granite blocks, hauled myself out, lost my balance, and fell backwards, crashing against the rock and jarring every bone in my body. For a moment the sky went black and a sound like low-flying aircraft zoomed through my befuddled brain. As I came to I felt sick, winded, and unsure if I'd be able to move again; lying there like an upturned turtle, held down by an overfull rucksack wedged among the rocks, my legs splayed out at strange angles. Far beneath me, as in the bowels of a glacier, I could hear water running.

Alan was ahead and out of sight, lost in his own personal misery of heat and weariness. Ignorant of my predicament he was unraveling the mysteries of this maze, and I had no voice with which to call for help.

Unbuckling the waist belt, I prayed that the sack would not plunge out of reach. Carefully wriggling out of the shoulder straps I managed to ease myself to a sitting position and check for broken bones. Nothing, thank God, but angry swellings on both legs, a raw elbow, and aches in sundry places. And sweat that stung my eyes.

We continued down together—soon on grass, then through minor gullies and out to grass again and a stream that was followed among a forest of thistles. The unmistakable fragrance of Spain now wrapped us in its bubble. Suddenly the heat was okay. It was Spanish heat. It belonged.

Stumbling into the Estós *refugio* we lined up the drinks on a table, and when they were empty took a bottle of rough red wine with us and continued upvalley in search of a favorite pine glade on a terrace above the river. Later, with a meal inside our bellies, the mountains black against the night sky, stars overhead, and the threat of another blue-sky day tomorrow, our day just gone slipped into perspective. Lumps, cuts, and bruises covered legs and arms. I ached all over. But that was alright. This is where I wanted to be. We'd paid our dues and arrived in one piece. Tomorrow we'd go climbing.

As the wine bottle passed between us, I heard Alan mumble: "Well, that was something of a doo-day." And I said "Amen" to that.

NO FRIEND IN HIGH PLACES

The Pyrenean High Route makes an epic traverse of the range from the Atlantic to the Mediterranean, keeping as close to the frontier ridge as possible. Since its inception by Georges Véron in the late 1960s there has never been one definitive trail—indeed, long sections have no visible trail at all—and there have been numerous variations, all leading to a challenging trek of about 42 days. In 1979, for his first visit to the Pyrenees, Pete Smith and I trekked a two-week section of the Haute Route, but with variations of our own. It proved to be another memorable trip, with tough days counterbalanced by laughter; but I hadn't considered his ability to embarrass . . . Pete and I had known each other for years, but this was our first mountain trip together. We laughed a lot, challenged each other with unbelievable stories, and shared the same ironic humor. A few days ago we were struggling out of the Aspe valley on a trail that had no respect for heavy sacks and weary legs; I was in front, suffering (momentarily, you understand) in the heat, when Pete, gauging how I felt, had summoned strength and breath and stormed past me, hands in pockets, whistling.

Now we were camped beside Lac de Pombie at the foot of Pic du Midi, the massive south-facing walls of the mountain softening in the alpenglow. It was my turn to cook the meal, and I was crouched in the porch of the tent protecting the cooker from a breeze when Pete, who was outside, announced that he could see a couple of climbers beside the refuge above us studying a copy of my guidebook. "I'll just go and tell them the author is down here," he said. "I'm sure they'll want to meet you!"

I gave him a mouthful of abuse.

The next morning it was our plan to move on to the Balaïtous massif, so we collapsed the tent, ambled up the slope to the refuge, then began our descent to the Ossau valley, across which the bold granite mountains were as tempting as ever. In another four hours or so we would be there, and I looked forward to introducing them to Pete, to crossing their ridges, skirting their lakes, and camping among their wild recesses once more. He'd find the Balaïtous very different from Pic du Midi and those mountains we'd traversed since leaving the Aiguilles d'Ansabère, but I was sure they'd be to his liking, rough and uncompromising as they are.

Descent to the valley is steep in places, but easy enough, and at one point there's a trail junction with a footbridge over a stream that takes one path into woodland. That would be our path, but standing at the junction were two climbers clutching a map and a copy of my guidebook. My heart sank.

"Are you lost?" asked Pete.

"Not really," answered one. "Just wondering which path to take."

"Don't you have a guidebook?" asked Pete, feigning innocence.

"Yeah, but it doesn't mention one of the options." He held the book up for Pete's attention.

"Blimey!" said Pete. "You're not using that, are you? I know old Reynolds. Full of bullshit, he is. As for the Pyrenees, he's only been here a couple of times. And that was by car. He never walks anywhere, lazy sod. But he's got a good imagination."

With that I left the three of them to discuss the merits of guidebooks and their authors, crossed the bridge and disappeared into the woodland. I'd get my own back later.

DEATH OF AN IZARD

Watching wildlife at ease in an untamed landscape adds a bonus to mountain days. In the Pyrenees we'd often catch sight of large birds of prey, hear the shrill whistle of marmots, and see small herds of the local chamois, known here as izard, grazing a distant hillside. Only once have I had cause to regret a close encounter with a wild creature, and that came in 1982.

After several days spent crossing a high country of rocks and scant vegetation, we came down into a green valley—green of grass, moss, and lichen; green of deciduous trees; and with a river running through that had side-channels enclosing deep green pools. There was also the novelty of a path to follow. True, it was narrow and faint in places, but a path all the same—not simply an animal track—and since it was aiming more or less where we wanted to go, we took it.

Locked into our own individual worlds, Alan and I had no need for conversation, and since the way was clear enough it was possible to drift through the valley and sample all it had to offer without distraction, without concentration. The warmth of Spain encouraged an unhurried pace; we didn't fight it.

The path squeezed between stands of birch, alder, and dwarf pine, then emerged to a natural meadowland, and there, just ahead, an izard slumbered beside the trail. We stopped immediately and took a couple of photographs before the animal came alert, trembling with fear. Its head swung this way and that, nostrils flaring to catch our scent.

Then it snorted, sprang to its feet, gave a frightened leap, and ran across the sloping meadow. Clearly something was wrong, though, for the creature stumbled, picked itself up, and turned a full circle before stumbling again and then limping towards the river.

Alan and I shrugged the rucksacks from our shoulders and took off after the izard. I reached it first, just as it fell onto a large rock wet with spray. Another step and it would have been in the water. Clutching the animal across the shoulders I eased it onto its side, felt its heart beating wildly in its chest, then noticed that its eyes were coated with a filmy membrane.

The izard was blind.

I stroked its flank, speaking softly in an attempt to calm its fears, leaned closer to see the eyes more clearly, when suddenly it jerked its head and the short scimitar-shaped horns brushed my face. At that moment I lost my grip and the izard sensed it, took advantage, and leapt away. Straight into the river.

The current was strong and swept the doomed creature downstream. It bobbed like a cork, but moments later it was dashed against a semi-submerged slab of rock. The izard scrabbled and stumbled and then managed to stand upright on the rock. For a brief moment it was safe. But the slab was an island; there was no escape, and we watched as the animal faltered, panicked, and slid back into the river.

The izard lost the fight, and the green, green valley lost its appeal.

AMONG THE ENCHANTED MOUNTAINS

On the Spanish slopes of the Pyrenees, south of Val d'Aran, the Parc Nacional d'Aiguestortes i Estany de Sant Maurici is a district of abrupt peaks, romantic secluded valleys, and rock-girt lakes. Near the eastern end of this national park stands a prominent twin-summited peak known as Els Encantats, often mirrored in the Sant Maurici lake. In the early hours of a damp September morning in 1978 Hugh Walton and I arrived on the outskirts of Espot, which serves as the gateway to these Enchanted Mountains.

Bleary-eyed and stale of mouth I peered through the tent doorway at clouds squatting on the treetops and a steady drizzle falling. It was not the most promising of mornings, but there was Hugh, clad in rain gear, eager for a day's activity; sorting ropes and slings, he was undeterred by the lack of evidence that there was anything at all to climb. Where had that optimism sprung from? We'd only met two days ago as a result of Mike phoning to say he couldn't make it to the Pyrenees after all, as he had to go to Tanzania, but he had a neighbor with a couple of weeks to spare who was looking for mountains he'd never climbed before.

Hugh had arrived in time for a meal and a few hours' sleep, then we'd set out; two strangers wondering what the other was thinking, how the coming weeks would pan out, and what we'd achieve—if anything. With foot hard down on the accelerator, we'd drive for exactly a hundred miles, then change places for another hundred, eating as we went, and stopping briefly only to fill up with petrol and to empty bladders. It was by far the quickest I'd ever traveled through France, crossing into Spain at midnight and creeping into the Espot campsite in the dead and dark early hours. Three hours' sleep is all we'd managed, yet there he was, eager to get started. With a mixture of foreboding and excitement I anticipated a busy fortnight.

Stumbling through the village that showed little sign of life, we continued on a stony track to the Sant Maurici lake. By the time we arrived there clouds were, if anything, lower and more dense than they'd been at the campsite, and it was still raining. Spanish rain, I'd discovered years before, is every bit as wet as rain at home, and inside rain gear, if you're heading uphill with rucksack and climbing gear, there's a tendency to overheat. We'd gained 2,000 feet since leaving the campsite and, pausing for a moment, Hugh unzipped his jacket and let the steam out.

On the journey through France he'd bombarded me with questions about the mountains, their routes, and grades. He wanted to know not just the highest peaks but the most interesting, their location, their history, which ones I'd climbed, what my plans were. Now we were at the lakeside, black and dreary on this gray, damp morning, he demanded to know where were these Enchanted Mountains I'd banged on about.

"This way," I said, and wandered towards pinewoods grouped below the unseen twin peaks that were icons of the district. The Enchanted Mountains were precisely that—Els Encantats, the Sierra de los Encantados. Erring shepherds turned to stone, their ankles at last came into view as we emerged from the dripping trees. A tongue of old snow fanned out below the central gully, and as we stood for a moment peering through the gloom, two young izard picked their way across it before disappearing in the mist.

"Might as well take a look," he said. "We've brought the rope this far; it'd be daft not to use it." And with that he set off, heading for the dark underside of the clouds.

This had not been on my agenda for a first climb with a complete stranger. I'd pictured scrambling on sun-bathed crags, eyeing each other up, wondering whether we'd achieve anything or fall out on Day One. But rain or no rain, Hugh clearly had other ideas. He was here to climb mountains, seen or unseen.

Bemused, I ran after him, wondering what was going through his mind. Unless he knew something of which I was unaware, how could he possibly decide to climb a mountain he'd never seen, could not see, and had no idea where any existing route might go? I at least had gazed on these impressive pillars before, but had never been close enough to even touch rock, let alone make an attempt to climb them. Now it seemed as though we'd be having a crack at them, for it was obvious that Hugh was uninterested in just peering into falling rain and gently swirling mist. Simply prospecting a route would not be enough for him; we were about to climb.

By reputation the Gran Encantat, the higher of the two summits, is not unduly difficult, and even by Pyrenean standards is of no great height, but it offers something like 2,600 feet of ascent, and for a first attempt it would at least be helpful to see what we were doing and where we were going. There was little to be seen, but we kicked our way up the snow slope anyway and stood momentarily at the foot of the gully. It looked steep to me, but that didn't impress Hugh. Letting more steam out of his jacket, he gestured at the fist-sized stones embedded in the snow, lowered his rucksack, and pulled on his helmet. We roped up without discussion, and with a grunt which I interpreted as meaning: "Mind if I lead?", he set off into the gloom.

Broken rock afforded plenty of holds as we progressed up the right-hand side of the gully, yet broken rock is broken rock, and some came my way, whizzing past in a shower of stones. Despite the occasional bombardment, and despite seeing nothing beyond vague shapes, my confidence grew as we surged our way through the clammy mist. Rain was no longer falling, but moisture was all around us. The air was damp; the slabs we climbed were cold and wet; water spilled over tiny ledges and dripped from unseen projections. Some grooves retained ice from last winter, and in one place we were forced to burrow through a water-carved tunnel. Hugh went first, his back pressed against the rock, knees tight against a tube of ice. Every sound echoed, and we inhabited worlds of our own. Time lost all meaning as we lost contact with the tongue of snow, the lake, and that other world down there.

"Down there" could have been fifty or fifteen hundred feet. If Hugh or I disturbed a stone it bounced and clattered—then nothing but silence. We could gauge nothing from that.

Rain returned, then fell as snow. Light flakes dusted the route with fine powder. Above us were more broken slabs, a ledge or two, a cleft, an overhang we could turn without trouble. We rarely spoke, for there was nothing to say. Hugh climbed smoothly. He was in his element—strong, safe, and confident—and I discovered that he'd been running climbing courses for several years in north Wales. Although he'd never been to the Pyrenees before, it was as though this were his home territory; he understood rock and all its subtleties, Spanish or Welsh. No wonder he looked happy as we arrived at the Enforcadura, the top of the gully at a sniff under 8,900 feet. We might have seen nothing yet, and there was little to see above us, but imagination took over.

Saying nothing about the more challenging alternative of the Petit Encantat, I nodded to the right. "Gran Encantat," I said. "Another hundred and fifty feet and we're there." For some reason that defeats my memory, we unroped. Hugh coiled it and fitted it to his rucksack.

"D'you mind?" he asked, nodding at the snow-dusted rock.

"Be my guest."

After a moment's examination he blew on his fingers, chose a line, and started up the right-hand slabs, leaving me to follow his lead once more. I was content with that, for he had seldom wavered in his route finding, and the calm deliberation employed on rock he'd never seen before was a joy to watch.

The route he chose may not have been the "normal" route. Who knows—or cares? He climbed straight up for several feet, then strayed to the right, moving onto what felt like exposed terrain, and as I moved after him the air quickened around me; a puff of wind whipped across my face and shredded the clouds. I glanced down, and for the first time that day I had a view—onto the lake of Sant Maurici, 2,600 feet below my feet.

Had we not been cocooned in mist all morning, had we been able to see what we were climbing and what was beneath us, had we grown used to a scene of distant peaks and lakes and pinewoods below, the sight of Sant Maurici looking no bigger than a puddle would not have come as such a shock. But none of those things had belonged to our climb, and for a moment I was unnerved.

Hugh must have sensed something too, for he looked down at me. "We'll tie on again," he said. I turned away from the view, found a comfortable stance, and when he'd uncoiled the rope and lowered an end to me I clipped on with trembling fingers. With that the clouds gathered around us once more, and we resumed our climb into the unknown.

-------------------▲-------------------

HOLE IN ONE

Hugh, I discovered, had an insatiable appetite for climbing. With each summit reached during that hectic fortnight in 1978, he'd point to a neighboring peak and demand to know its name, altitude, and history.

He'd spot a high point far off and want to climb it, so we raced from one massif to another, scrambled up gullies, chased along ridges and collected summits like manic Munro baggers. And when he caught sight of the Vignemale, with the longest glacier in the Pyrenees, he demanded we add it to our list. Little did he realize what that would lead to.

"So what happened to daybreak?"

It must have been at least two hours since he'd anticipated sunrise would happen within the hour, and there was no sign of it yet.

Hugh had left his watch at home, and mine had given up the ghost a couple of days ago, so we had no firm idea of time. Not that it mattered overmuch, but it would have been helpful now and then. Last night, for example, we'd discussed making our ascent of the Vignemale by way of the Ossoue glacier shortly after dawn, which would mean leaving our tent in the dark and using headtorches to find our way up the trail. "A little over an hour should do it," I'd told him. "Fine," he'd said. "We'll set out an hour before the sun comes up." Tapping the side of his head, he'd claimed to have an inbuilt clock. "I'll give you a call," he'd said. "Trust me."

Now we were seated upon lichen-cushioned rocks by the snout of the glacier eighteen hundred feet higher than our tent, and stars were still flashing in the black night sky. If sunrise were imminent, it was a well-kept secret.

I don't know how long we sat there, but dawn was a long time coming. So long, in fact, that I reckon he'd woken me some time before midnight; although we'd never know for certain. But when day did break at last it was spectacular, for as the mountains emerged from darkness, the valley in which Gavarnie lay far below now filled with cloud, with only the upper reaches of the Cirque wall standing clear. Streamers of sunlight—ranging from magnolia to a deep cherry red—flooded the sky and dazzled on the glacier beside us.

"Time to go," I said, desperate for activity, and we roped up.

Our route led up the left-hand side of the glacier below the Crête du Montferrat, and as I'd been on the mountain before I was happy for Hugh to take the lead and have the task of breaking trail through the fresh snow that covered the ice. There was a purity about that snow covering, but it also demanded caution as crevasses could be hidden by it. Because of that, Hugh probed the way ahead with his ice axe while I enjoyed the views.

It was a slow plod that morning, and after a while he grew weary of the glacier, for he much preferred to be on rock. "If it's not vertical," another climber once told me, "ice belongs in whisky." Perhaps Hugh sympathized with that notion. "What's that ridge like?" he asked, pointing off to our right. "Interesting, but not overly difficult," I told him, "with a monstrous drop down the north face on the far side."

I then proceeded to explain that there was a route across the summit of the Petit Vignemale that continued to Pointe Chausenque, beyond which it was necessary to descend to the glacier and cross the head of the Couloir de Gaube before tackling the final rocks of the main Vignemale summit, the highest point on the borders of France and Spain at 10,820 feet.

"How about it?"

"That's fine by me," I agreed.

"Then let's cut across the ice and get onto rock," he said.

Avoiding a hummock that protruded from the surface of the glacier to reveal layers of blue-green ice, he carefully worked his way towards the ridge that formed the glacier wall. Then suddenly he stopped and muttered: "I'm not sure I like this." And as he spoke I noticed he was sinking through the snow surface.

I just had time to slam in my ice axe and put a twist of rope round it, and when I looked up there was a neat hole about ten paces away, into which Hugh had disappeared. The rope was running after him, snatching coils from my hand, so I threw my weight on the axe, took the strain, and the rope stopped moving.

Somewhere in that hole Hugh would be swinging in a crevasse. I'd never had someone on my rope fall into a crevasse before, but I figured he was strong and experienced enough to climb out. After all, he had prusiks to hand, and I was certain he'd know how to use them, so I relaxed and took my time to study the view. It was a beautiful morning and I had it all to myself. There was no sign of other climbers on either the glacier or its bordering ridges, no recognisable sound disturbed the peace, no bird sailed above or below me. Nothing moved, save for the sun, which climbed slowly above the distant mountains, and Gavarnie's cloud-sea that started to evaporate as the day began to warm. My location on the glacier was perfect for a study of the frontier peaks, and I was content to put names to individual summits, ticking off in my mind those I'd summited in the past. So many held memories, and they'd never looked better than on this pristine morning.

But as time ticked by I began to wonder how Hugh would be faring in his crevasse, with a view somewhat less expansive than mine, but a situation rather more exciting.

Ignorant of the true passage of time, it seemed that I knelt on the ice for at least half an hour, but it was probably much less than that. There was still no sign of Hugh, and I speculated whether I should untie the rope and go home to inform his widow where his remains could be found.

Then I noticed a movement around the hole. The tip of an axe appeared. Then the top of a helmet. Hugh's face looked out at me; it was red from exertion. Then both head and shoulders were revealed.

"Hold it there," I suggested. "This will make a great picture."

And as I carefully composed my photograph, he spoke. Rather calmly, it seems, in retrospect.

"I shouldn't take too long if I were you," he said. "Only, from where I was swinging, I could see exactly where the crevasse is running. And you're standing right over the top of it."

THE LOST PATROL

In September 1980 I was once again in the Pyrenees with Pete Smith and Alan Payne, this time trekking from Gavarnie to Luchon, weaving from one side of the Franco-Spanish border to the other and either camping or sleeping in huts at the end of the day. We had the mountains to ourselves as we approached the heart of the range and entered Spain by the "back door" to make our way to Viados and its privately owned refugio.

Our approach to Viados was an unconventional one—the pass by which we'd crossed from France being rarely trod. But it had revealed the great block of the Posets massif in all its impressive beauty, and from that high point it was with us every step of the way. Never had this second highest of Pyrenean mountains looked more appealing.

The approach itself took us over verdant slopes dotted with pine and spattered with the rich greenery of alpenrose shrubs long out of bloom. We gorged ourselves on fat bilberries and juicy wild raspberries. And as we descended into the valley of the Cinqueta de la Pez hundreds of grasshoppers leapt in the air, disturbed by three pairs of well-worn boots. Here the warm fragrance of upland Spain was almost intoxicating. I could suffocate on it without complaint.

It was good to be back in Viados—that summer-only hamlet of mottled stone barns spread across the hillside—and the simple *refugio* that would be our home for the night with its direct view of those barns, with the slopes of Posets rising ever higher just across the way.

The guardian was preparing to close up in advance of the coming autumn. His season was over; he was going home, but we could use the two-room annex if we wanted—our washroom would be the log trough by the stream—and okay, he'd make a meal for us.

He had time. "Ha! There is time. I know the way downvalley in the dark. It's okay."

A donkey wheezed three times across the meadows. The mountains turned purple, and in minutes darkness fell.

We were called to the main building to eat, and by candlelight emptied a huge tureen of noodle soup between us, ate our fill from a platter of vegetables and a monster omelette stuffed with salami and tomatoes, and four times called for a refill of wine in the brown earthenware jug. The wine was thick as a bull's blood, and by the third glass my head was being clamped in a vice. We sat outside and counted stars.

The guardian was leaving. He beckoned to Pete and said he'd show him where to hide the key after we'd finished in the morning. From our bench, Alan and I watched with amusement as tall, long-legged Pete, with a quizzical smile on his face, attempted to walk a straight line to the annex alongside the Spaniard. Surely we hadn't drunk that much wine. Had we?

We were slow to move next morning, and three fuddled brains tried to remember where the key was to be hidden.

The rucksacks seemed extra heavy, the sun brighter than before, and the trail much steeper than I recalled from previous treks through the valley. Recently shorn meadows gave off their pungent aroma as we shuffled our way past the barns. Beyond them dried flowers were mixed with late-summer grasses. Beside the path plate-sized thistles spread their silver and yellow stars; crickets and butterflies drifted around us, and streams reflected the sunlight.

We gave up and lounged beside one of the streams. Wild mint was growing along its bank; I rubbed the leaves between thumb and forefinger and in an instant was transported to the Atlas Mountains where, long ago, Alan and I had first shared a rope. Now he too was taken there by the mint's unmistakable fragrance. I dipped my hat in the stream and let the water run down my face, and in moments felt more alive.

THE WAY TO ANDORRA

Sometimes Alan and I would pitch a tent in our chosen valley and spend two weeks on a concentrated climbing spree. Sometimes we'd drift from one massif to another—again, collecting summits and exploring hidden corries. But on other occasions we'd make a long trek from one railhead to the next, and that way we would cross passes, and wander through regions that would otherwise remain unknown to us. In 1982 we chose a route that would take us from Luchon to Andorra, from the Maladeta to the Coma Pedrosa. Once again, it seemed, we had the mountains to ourselves.

Since wandering through Salardú five days ago we'd seen no-one, for our route across the mountains had been devised to avoid habitation. Yes, we'd passed the occasional shepherd's hut and even walked through remnants of a stone-built hamlet now falling apart and being strangled by vegetation, but every building we'd seen had been deserted, save for an occupying force of lizards and butterflies. This was, surely, one of the last true wilderness areas of Europe, and we reveled in its remoteness.

In the evening we'd pitch our tent by a tiny lake or stream. Some of the lakes were black round the edges with tadpoles. We shared some of the streams with izard; some of the meadows with marmots. On ridges and high passes we'd dangle our legs over empty space and count lammergeyer, eagle, or buzzard, gazing south into blue sierras or north to green distant foothills. The mountains that rimmed every horizon were snow-free. There were no glaciers, no famous summits or dramatic pinnacles of rock to set a climber's fingers itching, but a lack of these was not to be regretted. In our chosen wild landscape every modest peak had its place; there was order in this Genesis land, and every one of our senses was saturated.

Hours would pass without conversation, but each mountain and valley had its own voice. The late-summer breeze carried the sound of water spraying over rocks, the rattle of dried grass and seedpods, the cry of a bird, the sound of a stone disturbed by an unseen animal. On the mountains we picked a way over unmarked rocks. In the valleys our legs brushed against shrub and dwarf tree. Spain bathed us in its warmth; we filled our lungs with air thick with the scent of a thousand aromatic plants.

Now we were nearing Andorra at the end of our two-week journey, and we both knew our days of solitude were coming to a close. A moorland spread around us, and for a moment my mind fled the Pyrenees and settled on the Carneddau in north Wales, where the coloring of vegetation was similar to this, although the fragrance was anything but. An easy pass took us out of Spain to grant a sudden view across a French valley to Andorran mountains. From it we descended over rocks to a small lake, and from the lake down into a green valley with a clear stream flowing through.

Later we came upon an ancient path, possibly a mule-trail, rising across a hillside towards an obvious saddle guarded by contrasting peaks—one sharply pointed, the other domed but appealing. The saddle marked our way into Andorra, and as we climbed towards it, a movement on the sharp right-hand peak caught our attention. With surprise we noted three neatly dressed climbers in matching outfits descending towards the pass. They arrived moments before we did. French, they were. French border police, making a rare visit to this remote mountain crossing.

"Bonjour," we said.

"Bonjour," they replied, before demanding to see our passports. These border police were delighted to see us. Alan and I may have seen no-one for five days, but they explained with expressive grins that we were the first foreigners they'd met on this pass in more than three years. To celebrate the fact, and as if to prove they were French, they produced bottles of red wine from their

rucksacks, and there, at over 8,000 feet above sea level, we did our best to further Anglo-French relations by having a party.

I remember nothing of our descent into Andorra.

RENDEZVOUS IN GAVARNIE

In 1980 I began to research the history of Pyrenean climbing and wrote to the brothers Ravier in Bordeaux for information. Although my French was negligible, and they spoke no English, they were extremely generous in supplying me with everything I could wish for. Not only were they the most talented climbers ever to concentrate on these mountains, their knowledge of them was encyclopaedic, and a friendship was forged that continues through the years. But we never met face to face until 2006.

Gavarnie's backdrop is spectacular. Rising more than 4,000 feet above the screes, a vast amphitheater wall is crowned by a group of 10,000 foot summits that carry the frontier ridge. Streaked with waterfalls and layered with terraces of snow and ice, the wall attracts climbers at the sharp end of the sport with extreme routes and seemingly impossible lines. The Cirque de Gavarnie is, of course, the cradle of Pyrénéisme.

So it seemed fitting that the *mairie* of this little roadhead township should organize a celebration of Pyrenean mountains and mountaineering, using as a focus the fiftieth anniversary of the first ascent of the north face of the Tour du Marboré, which is a prominent feature at the head of the valley and whose ascent had become a milestone in local climbing history. My invitation to the gathering came as a surprise—but, flattered by it, I caught a flight

to Pau, hired a car for a few days, and that evening bivouacked in a meadow with the outline of familiar mountains for company.

The following morning, with a couple of hours or so to kill before the celebrations were due to begin, I scampered up the trail beyond Gavarnie's churchyard to the Plateau de Bellevue, where my love for the Pyrenees began so many years ago. And there I settled upon a rock, breathless among the flowers, and gazed at the Cirque whose summits then wore a pillow of cloud sent up from Spain. From out of that cloud the Grande Cascade poured its misty stream, its message but a distant whisper carried by a stray breeze. All else was soundless.

Before midday I hoped to meet for the first time two brothers with whom I'd been corresponding for a quarter of a century. Jean and Pierre Ravier were to be the chief guests at the celebration; Jean had made that first ascent of the Tour du Marboré's north face fifty years ago, but he and his twin had been at the forefront of Pyrénéisme for decades and were now celebrating sixty years of top-grade activity there. Although we'd never met I knew their record, admired and respected them as much for their humility as for their achievements, and counted them as friends. Now I was excited by the prospect of meeting them at last. Excited, but nervous too.

Nervous? Well, yes. What if I were to be exposed as an impostor?

So far as climbing was concerned, Jean and Pierre were in a different league, a different universe. They were superstars at the very pinnacle of their sport, whereas I'd never been more than a scrambler, a stumbler and bumbler, a recorder of walks and modest climbs. What we had in common was a passion for the Pyrenees, a passion that had been expressed time and again in the letters, cards and gifts of books and photographs that journeyed between us year after year. Although language could have been a barrier between us, the Pyrenees were a unifying force.

I hoped that would be enough to continue our friendship once we'd met face to face.

Gazing at the Cirque from my perch on the Plateau de Bellevue, I remembered so well that first visit almost forty years ago—the late-lying snow, with soldanellas that seemed to burn their way through; cornices picked out by the sun on the Pics d'Astazou across the way; the moon rising over the mountains and washing them with its silvery light. I thought of camps and bivouacs, the friends with whom I'd shared a rope, and recalled numerous occasions when I'd crossed through the great cleft of the Brèche de Roland from France to Spain and vice versa, summiting peaks by their "normal" routes—never by their extreme faces—unlike Jean and Pierre whose record was unassailable . . . Reality took over as I emerged from clouds of memory, for it was time at last to meet these two prophets of Pyrénéisme. I'd have to move, or I'd be late.

Setting off at a jog I took a different route down to the valley, leaping streams and dodging the flowers. Soon among trees, I slalomed between pine, birch, and alder on a trail that brought me at last into a large open meadow and the track that leads to Gavarnie. The street was beginning to fill. Not with donkeys and ponies for tourists to ride as far as the Hôtellerie du Cirque near the foot of the Grande Cascade, but with a babble of climbers from both sides of the frontier and spanning several generations. They all seemed so confident, so at home. Everyone appeared to know everyone. I knew no-one.

At the far end of the street a large man with a shock of dark hair and a blue sweatshirt stepped in front of me.

"Monsieur Reynolds?" he asked. I nodded, for I'd run out of breath and was panting hard. "The brothers Ravier are waiting for you. Please come with me."

I wanted to ask his name and how he recognized me, for I'd never seen him before. Who was he? But he was walking away and I was breathless, so I followed, wheezing. Moments later we reached the junction not far from the Maison du Parc. Sweat was running down my face; I needed a wash and to change my clothes, but it was too late, for there stood the two brothers it had taken me 25 years to meet. Beside them stood Michèle, Jean's wife, who speaks English and would be able to translate.

There were no common words between Jean, Pierre, and me, beyond a shy "Bonjour," so we stood in the street and simply beamed at one another. But the Pyrenees has its own language, which the three of us understood so well. After all these years our friendship was safe.

....

A version of this story was published in *The Alpine Journal* 2007.

ALPS

Always Something New to Discover

A year after returning from the Atlas Mountains I went to the Alps for the very first time, and was so inspired by what I saw that I went back a few months later to work in the Engadine valley on the edge of the Bernina massif. Watching the seasons unfold on the mountains and in the valleys became an ongoing education, and even now, several decades later, the Alps continue to work their magic. They may be the world's best-known mountains, with every valley and summit explored, mapped, photographed and described, but there's always something new to discover, and each day spent among them leads to an enrichment of the senses.

Writing and photographic assignments have enabled me to visit every district, from the Alpes Maritime to the Julians of Slovenia, and for a number of years I organized and led walking holidays among some of the most scenically dramatic places in the Alps. There have been few summits but plenty of passes. Days, weeks, and months have been spent devising and researching routes of varying length and complexity until virtually the whole range has become familiar.

For a century and more, gray-beards and pundits have decried the overrun of the Alps by tourists, complaining of overcrowded valleys, the desecration of mountains and landscapes by railway, road, and cableway. But in almost fifty years of Alpine wandering I've discovered scores of pristine, seemingly untouched districts as visually exciting as those that feature on every calendar and chocolate box lid. It's true that the path less trod is almost always worth taking.

Familiar, but always rewarding, the Playground of Europe retains the power to excite. And I guess it always will. Stories in this section date from 1967 onwards, and the incidents and experiences described took place in many different regions and in all seasons.

A BIG MOON RISING

Winter in the Alps. Coated with snow from base to summit, the mountains appear to be even higher than they are in reality. During the coldest days in the valley hoar frost thickens every twig, while dense baskets of snow are suspended from the branches of larch trees. The four lakes spread across the valley floor between St Moritz and Maloja are hidden by a thick covering of ice. The temperature plummets the moment the sun goes down, but despite the cold in February 1967 I had a dream to fulfil. A crazy dream, perhaps, but a romantic notion had taken over and sanity was left behind . . . In retrospect it's clear that Noldi didn't want me to do it, but he was reluctant to say so. Despite his eccentricities, not even he would consider camping near the summit of an 11,000 foot mountain in the middle of winter. And he had been born in the valley. Perhaps that's it. He knew how cold it would be, knew the fickle nature of an Alpine winter, and, having been involved with his neighbor in avalanche rescue, knew too that a big dump of snow could have a devastating effect on the upper slopes of almost any mountain. A couple of days ago we'd had a big dump of snow.

• • •

So he prevaricated, found reasons to delay my departure. When I told him I was happy to walk the few miles to the base of Piz Corvatsch, he would hear none of it. "I'll take you in the car," he insisted. "Just give me a couple of minutes, and we'll go."

The afternoon dragged by. It would be the first and only time that winter that I'd have the night off, so I wanted to make the most of it. Yet Noldi, my boss, fiddled about and bustled from one room to another with his delaying tactics. "Won't be a moment," he'd say, then disappear for ten minutes.

But at last he indicated we could go, dumped my rucksack into the back of his Opel estate, and off we went, the snow chains clickety-clacking along the icy road that led to Champfèr and Silvaplana, then on a causeway between frozen lakes to Surlej and the Corvatsch cable-car station. He wished me well, then sped away before I'd entered the building.

The place was deserted. There was no queue of skiers full of anticipation; no buzz of excited voices. I was virtually alone, and it only struck me later that Noldi had timed his departure perfectly, for the girl cashing up at the ticket desk shook her head and told me the last run of the day had just set off.

"But I don't want to ski," I explained. "I want to camp on the mountain."

"Excuse me," she said. "Did you say you want to camp?"

I nodded.

"Camp!" she said, more to herself than to me. "Camp! On Piz Corvatsch?"

"That's right. I've got all I need," and indicated my rucksack.

The girl shook her head, and without taking her eyes off me picked up a telephone and gabbled away in Schwyzerdütsch. Although I couldn't understand much of what she said, several phrases were repeated.

Eventually she put the phone down and asked, "Just for one night, sir?" (Did I detect a touch of sarcasm?) "You have permission to ride the car with the refreshments," she announced. "It will leave in about ten minutes."

I paid for a one-way ticket, and fifteen minutes later swung into the air along with several crates of beer, schnapps, and soft drinks. The Italian attendant glanced at my rucksack with the tent rolled on top, then looked away with the expression of a man who'd just witnessed an accident and wished he hadn't.

It's bitterly cold at 10,800 feet in February, and with the sun sinking fast and shadows racing up the slopes of the mountain, it was going to be a lot colder soon, so once out of the cable car I headed up the ridge towards the summit, sucking icy air into my lungs as I laboured first through knee-deep, then thigh-deep snow. Some way above me I could see a large exposed rock, and figured it would do perfectly.

The snow was not as deep on the eastern side of the rock, so I began to clear a site with the ice axe, then stomped back and forth to make a level and fairly firm surface for the tent. Once that was up, I realized it was dark. And several degrees colder than when I'd started out almost an hour ago. My beard was a stiff wedge of crusted ice, and the warm glow of exercise was replaced by a chill that went right to the bone.

Inside the tent, huddled in my inadequate three-seasons sleeping bag spread over Noldi's airbed, I melted a billy of snow and made myself a hot drink. It took forever, but I had plenty of time for I'd be going nowhere until morning, and anticipation helped combat the cold. You see, I had this romantic notion to witness a full moon casting its light on big mountains. Not from below, but from a high vantage point; to be part of the scene, not simply to witness it. Snowdonia, the Lakes, the Scottish Highlands—they'd all provided rewards, but now I was working in the Alps the opportunity was too good to miss. Never mind the cold, that would add to the magic. Or so I told myself.

After an hour or so I crept out of the tent, groped my way onto the rock and peered into the Engadine valley, whose frozen lakes and twinkling lights were 1 mile below me. The valley ran south-westward, plunged into the darkness of Val Bregaglia, and beyond Piz Badile slid into Italy. North of my perch, St Moritz cast gems of light beside its lake and up the slopes behind the town. I wondered what Noldi was thinking, whether he regretted not taking me to Surlej even later than he had.

Then I turned to the other side of the mountain, where Val Roseg was a deep trench below the sharp tooth of Piz Roseg and the unmistakable shape of Piz Bernina. A flimsy wisp of cloud was draped across the face of both mountains that seemed close enough to touch. And there was the moon in all its silver fullness, rising out of some far-off anonymous valley. Unstoppable, it rose without obstruction. Shadows formed on west-facing slopes; summits and ridges glistened; distant peaks—too small to identify—were picked out by the lunar spotlight as the moon climbed higher and moved towards me.

The cold stabbed at fingers and toes. It ran up my arms and legs, and although my cheap down jacket was good enough for the valley, it was no match for this altitude. I shivered uncontrollably, but was reluctant to tear myself from the scene. The Alps were being revealed in all their winter glory by the all-powerful moon—the moon that would turn tides and measure years, control some folks' moods and call others to worship—and hold me in its spell as it drifted slowly across the night sky and turned darkness into light.

Suddenly I heard voices and, shuffling away from the rock, caught sight of a snake of flaming torches carving S-bends down the mountainside. I remembered, then, that this night of the full moon was being celebrated by a group of skiers making a torch-light descent of Piz Corvatsch led by local guides. It didn't last long, for the chorus of yelps and cries of excitement grew faint and the flaming torches disappeared, leaving me alone with the moonlight and the snow-covered mountains, content with the solitude.

At last the cold forced me back into the tent, into my sleeping bag and the chore of melting more snow for another hot drink. The big moon rising had been a spectacle worth seeing, and my tent would glow for a few more hours as it sailed overhead. Next would be sunrise, and that should be every bit as spectacular from here.

But when night had run its course there was no sunrise. Instead the tent threatened to collapse under the weight of new snow as the full moon disappeared to herald not another clear day, but a blizzard and white-out conditions. This was not what I'd anticipated. Descent in this would be an epic.

Perhaps Noldi was right after all.

▲

LIVING IN THE CLOUDS

As a result of spending countless weeks roaming the Alps over almost half a century, I have formed a number of lasting friendships with local people. They add much to every subsequent visit as we share a coffee, chew the cud, and quietly watch clouds drift across the mountains. It was in 2008 that we met Silvia after she'd written to me out of the blue, inviting us to call on her next time we were in the neighborhood. I'm so glad we did.

Our friend Silvia lives in the clouds. Not permanently, you understand, but occasionally, when a cold front moves in, or when there's a clash of temperatures as warm air rises from the valley to meet the colder air of the mountains. It's then that Silvia's world contracts, when visibility drops to just a few paces, and sounds are amplified. It's then that she needs to have a settled mind and a focus to her days.

Silvia tends cows for a living. Up there in the clouds she has charge of 67 cows and calves, a couple of horses, and four hens.

And a dog for company. In June each year when the snow of Switzerland is receding, she leads the animals from her village on one side of the valley to the lonely alp hut on the other. Sounds simple. But the valley is a deep one, steep-walled too, and a brisk walk from village to alp without animals would take most of us the best part of a day. Imagine doing that with a herd of cows. How long would that take, I wonder?

The solitary building in which she spends the summer, more than 5,900 feet up, is one-third home, two-thirds cattle byre and wood store. It has no running water. For that she takes her bucket to a spring-fed trough one hundred and fifty feet away. Her toilet is a "long-drop" in a timber housing behind the hut, and her meals are cooked on a wood-burning stove. But when the sun shines she has electricity, thanks to a small solar panel fitted to the roof. She has a solar shower too—a rubber bag filled with water which she hangs on the side of the building to catch the warmth of the sun. Simple, but effective, so she says.

We arrived at Silvia's alp on a morning when visibility was good and underlined her claim to have one of the finest views in all Switzerland. Whichever direction we looked, we gazed on mountains, valleys, and pastures. There were snowfields and glaciers, waterfalls and dark patches of forest on hillsides far away. Some slopes were crimson with alpenrose; others were blotched with cloud shadows. Spires of rock gestured into the blue; a craggy ridge curved to enclose a valley whose depths we could only guess. Screes tumbled in a motionless cascade at the head of a distant grassland. And cowbells rang a familiar theme tune.

On that first visit we fell in love with the alp, and with Silvia— for she called us in, sat us down, poured a drink, and percolated with delight at the day, the views (which she'd known all her life), and the seventeen chamois that came down to share the salt-lick with her cows. So we stayed. She made up a couple of low, simple beds and gave us a porcelain bowl in which to wash. The bedside table was an upturned log with a candle perched upon it. Outside the window, beyond the grazing cattle, the chamois and the hens, a mighty snow-caked peak of nigh-on 13,000 feet soared into a fleet of sail-like clouds.

Later the clouds came down, views were lost, and rain thundered on the roof. Silvia let some of the younger calves and their mothers into the byre. She removed the bells from around their necks, but one refused to cooperate, so she stuffed the bell with an old newspaper to deaden the sound. Night was a rumble of movement, rubbing, nuzzling, and lowing. And going out to visit the long-drop meant wading through a rich quagmire of mud and manure.

A week later I was in Austria, involved in work for the tourist authorities. They put me in a four-star hotel with all mod-cons, impeccable hygiene, and attentive staff. But I'd have given it all for Silvia's home in the clouds.

CHASING SUNRISE

The summer of 1967, my last as a single man, was spent in Austria leading mountain holidays. In each of my groups there would be two or three walkers who were especially tuned to the mountain world and eager for new experiences. One new experience I'd offer was the opportunity to bivouac on a local summit to capture the magic of sunrise. Every occasion was special—for each of us.

Mornings begin early in June when nights are at their shortest, and we were ready for this one. The evening before had been loud with crickets and the bellowing of marshland frogs at the end of the lake as we left the valley to begin our unhurried ascent of the mountain.

Even after night had fallen the forest path was so familiar that no torchlight was needed to find the way. It was no surprise, then, that we were on the summit by midnight, with a sky so thick with stars that you'd swear they were bright enough to cast shadows.

It was not much of a mountain, for it failed to reach even 7,000 feet. Here, location was everything. Standing clear of any neighboring peak, it won a panoramic view of great extent, for all the Eastern Alps were spread out for inspection. Not that we could see much detail at first—simply a blurred wash of pale cream where snow peaks stood rank upon rank in the distance, with vague shapes, gray on gray and a black intensity of rock face, and grass-covered hills much closer. Any wished-for detail would be revealed only when the new day dawned. Until then we crouched against a tiny chapel that crowned the summit and, without sleeping bags for comfort, spent the next few hours waiting for the stars to fade.

At 4am the sun exploded from a far-off valley to cast its glow across those eastern mountains, flooding the world with a temporary palette of color and staining valley mists with a delicate shade of pink. It was a welcome sight that I knew would last no more than a few brief minutes, so after soaking it all in we ran down the broad ridge, losing height as fast as we could, until the sun was hidden and we could wait a moment for a second dawn.

That dawn was every bit as good as the first, but we had a chance to win yet another sunrise if we continued our descent now. So off we went again, racing through pre-dawn shadows, over rocks and patches of old snow, then down a steep grass slope where, breathless, we waited half a minute—no longer than that—to capture our third sunrise of the morning.

Now we had time to fully appreciate the wonders of the moment, and stood there in no hurry to move, listing peaks and dreaming adventures for other days before continuing down the slope at a more leisurely pace, at last, towards the uppermost farm whose heavy beams were, it seemed, as old as the hills from which they'd been hewn. As we approached, the farmer's wife appeared at the door, her face bathed with early sunlight.

"Grüss Gott!"

She showed no surprise. "Where did you come from?" she asked. I told her, and told her about the three separate dawns.

"They were good?"

"Wunderschön!"

Having been invited to share her breakfast, we carried a table onto the verandah as her husband emerged from the cattle byre with a pail of warm milk. We ate home-made bread spread with home-made butter and jam, and drank coffee thick with the freshest milk in all Austria.

"Isn't this a bit early to be up and working?" I asked. (A stupid question, in retrospect.)

The woman smiled, reached across the table and, mother-like, placed her hand on my arm. The hand was blotched with age and stringy with raised veins, her fingers like the talons of a bird of prey.

"We have no clock," she told me. "When the sun warms our room, we get up."

....

A shortened version of this appeared in *Walking in Austria*, published by Cicerone in 2009.

---------- ▲ ----------

OUT WITH A PRO

A long relationship with the Austrian National Tourist Office has provided many opportunities over the years to walk and climb in the Eastern Alps whilst researching material and taking photographs for a variety of brochures. In 2008 I was back again on another commission that led to my working with a guide.

The moment I saw the gleam in Fredi Bachmann's eyes, I knew we'd get on. He had the look of a mountain man and the spark of someone earning a living doing what he loved best. Raised in the Glemmtal, he explained that at the age of nine or ten, he and a friend vowed they would climb every summit around their valley. Thirty years on, he was still climbing them with the same boyish enthusiasm. No, they're not big mountains in the Alpine scale of things, but altitude is not everything to those who love the hills. Neither is difficulty nor danger, and because of the passion he maintained for his valley, Fredi was the perfect choice of a guide for my time there writing text for a summer brochure. The man at the tourist office had insisted I take a guide. I'm glad he did. It would cost me nothing, and the experience proved invaluable.

Rain, then, was no deterrent as we set out that first day, and by the time we were halfway to the ridge above the village that rain had turned to snow. Fredi paused now and then to describe a plant that flowered in June, to tell me where to find salamanders, or to point out where only last year a golden eagle had nested—then we plodded on in reduced visibility to reach a large wooden cross marking a summit whose features were lost in what was now a complete white-out. Fredi was unconcerned. And in his company, so was I.

The next morning dawned with a sharp frost, clear blue sky and fresh snow lying above 5,000 feet. Above that level September was full of pretence for January.

Fredi arrived by the time I'd finished breakfast. "Let's go," he said. "The mountains are waiting." Ten minutes later we rode a gondola to the Schattberg and stepped out into a winter wonderland devoid of other people. The air was crisp, but sunlight dazzled on snow, and every summit as far as the eye could see appeared to have grown overnight by at least 3,000 feet. Individual massifs of the Northern Limestone Alps were plastered with snow; their abrupt south-facing walls had been stippled a creamy-white, with summits and ridges sharply outlined against the blue.

"This way," said Fredi, as he took off on an unseen path to skirt below the Westgipfel, where we gazed upon a small herd of chamois, then rose through a frost garden—hummocks of snow-covered grass and rocks frozen into extraordinary stems and flowers of hoar frost. Pure magic!

The modest Stemmkogel was our first summit, but moments later we were off again, our mutual excitement with the day spurring us on as we swooped down the ridge and, without altering our pace, went straight up again to the crown of the Saalbachkogel. "Where next?" I panted. "There," said Fredi, pointing to a higher crest that promised views of the Hohe Tauern. "Let's go."

Together we ploughed through knee-deep powder to a black lake lying below the Hochkogel. Two more chamois pranced across a precipitous slope nearby as we climbed the mountain's east ridge and gazed across a fluff of cloud floating in valleys, beyond which some of Austria's highest mountains gave a suggestion of the Himalaya. "The Hohe Tauern," said Fredi with what could have been taken as a hint of ownership (he'd climbed most of those peaks too). Among those mountains the Grossglockner was at the top of the hierarchy, but the elegant spike of the nearer Kitzsteinhorn held our attention more than any other. "Over there," he directed my gaze elsewhere. "Look, the Grossvenediger—superb!" Fredi gave voice to memory, while I simply day-dreamed.

Over the Hochkogel's summit we continued to the Hoch Saalbergkogel, whose ice-crusted ridges gave an interesting scramble, then across the easy domed Medalkogel, disturbing four ptarmigan that scurried away with a cackle of insults. Without realising it, we were collecting 'kogels' like unapologetic list-tickers, and as we did, Fredi would regale me with stories, facts and legends. These summits were as familiar to him as were his neighbors living down in the valley. Yet no amount of familiarity could deaden his enthusiasm.

By mid-afternoon we'd begun our descent, which brought us to the snowline and an isolated farm that in summer doubles as a restaurant. The farmer's wife brought us mugs of hot chocolate and strudel, and as we ate an older woman entered the room and, spying Fredi, drifted across to speak to him. But when she saw me, her eyes glistened and her cheeks puckered into a smile of recognition. "Grüss Gott!" she said. "Welcome back. Where is your group?"

Fredi turned to me with a frown. "You know each other?"

I nodded, slightly embarrassed to admit it. Then the truth tumbled out. For several summers I'd led mountain holidays based in the Glemmtal and neighboring valleys, had often climbed the same summits I'd shared with Fredi that day, and invariably brought my group to this alp farm for a drink on the way back down to our hotel.

"Why didn't you tell me?" he demanded.

"Simple," I said. "If you knew I'd been here before, you wouldn't have taught me half as much as you have. Acknowledging ignorance is the first step to learning."

------------▲------------

BATTLE OF THE IBEX

In the autumn of 1970, less than two years after I'd finished working in the Engadine valley, I was back for a short holiday—to visit friends, renew acquaintance with the mountains and to experience once more the wonders of sunset and sunrise as seen from an Alpine summit. Piz Languard, above Pontresina, may be modest in height and "a mere walker's mountain," but it's a great vantage point from which to study the Bernina massif, and it was high on my list.

Perched some 250 feet below the summit of Piz Languard, the Georgy hut was buzzing with voices when I arrived that September evening to be greeted by the guardian with a less than enthusiastic welcome. "There is no room," he growled. "We are full; no beds. You should have made a reservation."

"I don't need a bed," I told him. "Just a drink. That's all."

"It will be dark before you are halfway down to Pontresina." His attitude was disdainful, and the look on his face spoke more than words. Taking the hint I stooped to pick up my rucksack and slung it on my shoulder.

"I'm not going down tonight," I said. "Forget the drink. I'm going up."

He followed me out the door. "Where are you going?" he demanded.

"Up, I said, to the summit. That's where I'll spend the night."

"Zum Gipfel? There is no shelter on the summit!" Then his voice softened: "Look; come back. I will find a space for you somewhere."

But I was on my way and called over my shoulder, "I told you—I don't need a bed. I have all I want on my back."

At a little over 10,500 feet Piz Languard is an easy mountain, with a path all the way to the top. But evening was slipping away when I arrived there, and larchwoods down in the valley lost their autumn gold as the sun fell towards a distant horizon. Removing the tent from my rucksack, in a very short space of time I had it erected among the rocks with one guy tied to an ugly iron tripod that crowned the summit.

In time to capture the magic of sunset, I watched as the snowy symmetrical perfection of Piz Palü blushed and outshone her more distinguished neighbor, Piz Bernina. Between the two stretched the lovely Bellavista ridge, with Piz Zupò, Piz Argient, and the Crast'Aguzza, with the Swiss-Italian border picked out by a fading rim of pink. All those mountains across the way had become familiar during the months that I'd worked in the valley. Their ridges, faces, glaciers, and snowfields had been a backdrop to my days, and instinctively my gaze now panned from one alpenglow-bronzed summit to another. Yet so speedily was the sun disappearing that I was unable to identify more than a handful before twilight took over.

Using my sleeping bag as a cushion I sat on a summit rock, feet dangling over the side, and absorbed the peace of a world that seemed to be holding its breath. Mountains filled every horizon; those in the distant west were unreal cut-outs, black against the fading embers of the day. All was still, and alone on the summit I had all I could possibly want.

It wasn't the most comfortable of sites on which to pitch a tent, and a stray wind came from nowhere to rattle among the rocks, but I slept well enough and needed the alarm to wake me half an hour before dawn. It was still dark, but I heard voices and saw two pinpricks of light weaving from the south. Clearly some of those who'd spent the night at the hut were coming to watch sunrise from the summit. Unaware of my presence, they stopped a few paces below the actual top of the mountain. Huddled in down jackets they stamped their feet to keep warm, so I leaned out of the tent and called down to them.

"Would you like to come in out of the wind?"

It was still too dark to see the surprise on their faces, but the two Swiss women from Zürich were happy with the offer, and they squeezed inside to join me, chattering with excitement. And there we stayed until the stars went out and the first hint of daybreak streaked the eastern sky, gradually revealing mountains far off in Italy. Could that be the Ortler? We crawled outside then to witness yet another sunrise.

At home we sleep through too many summer dawns, but in the mountains I capture as many as possible. The magic is a daily occurrence, but each one is different. This one, this sunrise experienced from the summit of Piz Languard, was unbeatable for the immensity of the panorama and the sheer number of mountains on show. Last night I'd seen Piz Palü's three buttresses glowing on their western edges; now it was their east flanks that burned. Exposed rock on Piz Bernina took on the color of blacksmith's iron, while snowfields bled. As far as the eye could see the new day was being welcomed by individual peaks—first the highest, then their lower neighbors, while valleys still held on to night. Then, when the stain of sunrise had softened and all the Alps had been exposed, the women descended to the hut for breakfast, leaving me alone to brew a hot drink, nibble bread and cheese, and collapse the tent.

Rather than descend the normal way, I chose to work along the northwest ridge, and it wasn't long before the peace of the new morning was broken by a sound like two pieces of wood being beaten one against the other. Peering down into the shadowed face of the mountain I could just make out what had to be two ibex with their knobbly scimitar-shaped horns clashing in battle. Foreshortened by the angle, and unclear in the shadows, the creatures slipped in and out of my vision. But this was too good to miss, so I secured my sack on the ridge and picked a way down the rocks, careful to keep well to one side of the animals until I found myself below them.

Slowly I made my approach, barely breathing, camera held ready to capture their silhouette against the sky. The face of the mountain was steep, but holds were plentiful as I crept closer and closer. Suddenly I was aware of being surrounded by a herd of maybe nine or ten of the stocky animals. Nonchalantly picking among the rocks, most were unconcerned by the two males that battled for the right to dominate this year's rut. If any interest was shown, it was of this unusual shape moving among them.

Their musky smell was heavy in my nostrils. Their sneezing, snuffling, and grunting mingled with the slither of stones and the clash of the titans above. Wherever I turned ibex were within reach, and bulging eyes met my gaze. If only the light were better—what photos I'd capture! But no photographs could match these moments of reality; this was not a two-dimensional experience. In the confused light my presence was accepted. I was not a threat.

Then suddenly the sun flashed across the ridge and shone against the lens of my camera, and in an instant I was alone on the mountainside. All that told of moments before was a minor avalanche of stones and a rising cloud of dust.

REFLECTIONS IN THE ALPENGLOW

Having spent much of the summer of 2003 guiding walkers around several different Alpine regions, I checked my last group of the year onto their flight home and then took off for a solo tour of the Silvretta and Rätikon mountains, which straddle the borders of Austria, Switzerland, and Liechtenstein. Scrambling over ridges, I lazed on sun-warmed summits and celebrated the luxury of being alone hour after hour. But most evenings I'd descend to a hut for an ice-cold beer and a meal, and to meet others who shared my love of the high places.

The limestone wall of the Rätikon Alps softened in the slow, lingering dusk. Seated on the hut terrace I was served my meal, with finches chittering in the pine grove nearby. One flew to an upper cone, perched there, threw back its head, and called to the dying sun. Another answered. On this, my first visit to these mountains I'd spent several days wandering alone over meadow, ridge, and summit in an orgy of pleasure, and the finch's song gave voice to my satisfaction.

Meal over, shadows were swallowing screes when I went for a stroll to ease muscles taut from a long day over rough ground. Heading across a neighboring alp, then along a path under turrets catching the alpenglow, I turned a corner and came face to face with a tanned octogenarian in cord breeches with red braces, checked shirt, and Tyrolean felt hat, who looked as though he'd emerged from a 19th-century painting by ET Compton. His pale, watery eyes shone, his leathery skin folded into innumerable creases, and a day's white stubble bristled his chin.

"Is this not the most wonderful of evenings?" he demanded in a breathless German dialect.

I agreed that it was, and for ten minutes or so we shared a common delight in the slumbering mountains and their gullies, the valley, the chaos of boulders at the foot of the screes, the alpenroses, streams, a small green pool, and the rim of dwarf pines that outlined a nearby moraine. He had known 60 or more Alpine summers in his 80-plus years, yet his enthusiasm was as fresh as that of a 16-year old. It lit his features and bubbled from every pore, and I noticed, when we parted, a surprising spring to his step, as though by sharing his love of life he'd been rejuvenated.

....

This piece first appeared in *Alpine Points of View*, published by Cicerone in 2004.

THE WIND OF RELIEF

Ever since the Alps began to attract recreational walkers and climbers, local authorities have worked hard to create and maintain paths that allow travel from one valley or village to the next, from hut to hut, and even to the summit of some modest mountains.

Sometimes natural obstacles such as a cliff face, a raging torrent or a heavily crevassed glacier provide a challenge, and in the case of the ridge that divides Arolla from the Val des Dix that challenge has been overcome by the fixing of a ladder to the rock face—or, to be precise, three ladders. In 2001, those ladders seemed to be a challenge too far for a member of the group I was leading on behalf of a UK magazine.

"I'm nae gwin up there!" She turned away, shaking her head. "Naw wae m'I gwin up there!"

"You'll be alright," I tried to reassure her. "There's nothing to it. They're safe enough, sturdy, dependable. No problems."

"Ah het ladders. Het them!" she repeated.

The last time I'd crossed the Pas de Chèvres above the Cheilon glacier there had been two ladders. But there had since been further rockfall exposing a lower section of slab, and a third steel ladder had now been bolted to the rock face. Admittedly, a first glance could be a little off-putting, but the rest of the group seemed comfortable enough—or if not, they were putting on a brave face. Only wee Annie, the tiny woman from Dundee, was so intimidated as to voice her feelings. And she was adamant. She was not going up there. No way.

That morning we'd come over the neighboring Col de Riedmatten, a higher and rockier pass in the ridge dividing Arolla's valley from that of the wild and seemingly remote Val des Dix, then crossed the glacier on the way to the Dix hut for lunch in full view of the great triangular north face of Mont Blanc de Cheilon. It had been a relaxing time, seated on the terrace in the sunshine after a bowl of soup and a cold drink. But now we were on our way back to our base in Arolla, and I'd thought the alternative crossing via the Pas de Chèvres ladders would add a certain spice to the day.

Wee Annie thought otherwise.

With a sly wink to me, her husband took her to one side and had a quiet word. What he said, or the promises he gave her, I'll never know, but eventually she calmed down and, with my vow to stay close and safeguard every step, she reluctantly agreed to give it a go. So I sent the rest of the group up first while Wee Annie chewed on a Mars bar and was distracted by the view upvalley.

When the last of the group had disappeared over the ridge, I helped her onto the bottom rung, put my hands on the ladder either side of her arms and talked her up the first few steps. The ladders were near-vertical, and in places the rock face bulged so much that the rungs were flush against it, making it impossible for more than just the very tips of our boots to stay on them. But, remaining just two rungs below, I let her know that even if she slipped, she'd not fall because I was right behind her. Whether that was a comfort, I don't know, for she spoke not a word all the way up, only giving a soft grunt or a whimper now and then, and I sensed she was trembling with nerves for her legs and arms were shaking.

"Don't look down," I told her. "Or up. Just keep your eyes on the rungs, take your time, and we'll soon be there."

Moving to the second ladder was straightforward, for it was merely an extension of the first. But this one was much, much longer and, to Annie at least, it must have seemed an eternity that we spent moving slowly up it.

"You're doing fine. Nice and slowly, one step at a time."

Briefly looking down, I noticed the chaos of rocks and boulders between the foot of the ladders and the glacier were becoming much smaller as we approached a ledge projecting from the rock face, and I was glad that Annie was not so inquisitive. She would have flipped.

At the top of the second ladder I helped her to get onto the ledge and grasp the rungs of the much shorter top ladder. At any other time I'd have paused here to enjoy the view downvalley, but my duty was to help the tiny Scotswoman reach the Pas de Chèvres in safety, so up we went again; one step, then another. A whimper, then a grunt, and we were climbing higher. Annie's husband peered over the ridge and gave the thumbs up. "Good gel," he called. "Nearly at the top."

A few more rungs, a few more grunts and whimpers, and at last Annie stepped off the ladder onto the ridge.

Her relief was obvious, for all the nervous tension of the last ten minutes gave way, and into my unsuspecting face Wee Annie broke wind—and the trumpeting sound echoed across the valley.

MELLO MAGIC

I guess we all have our favorite places, but when it comes to the Alps it's not easy to choose one above all others. Some are favored for their outstanding beauty; others for the challenge of their peaks or for a particular dramatic feature. Some stand out because they hold recollections of days well spent among them. In the Italian Bregaglia there's a valley celebrated among climbers for its impressive granite walls, and it was a memory of that particular valley that called two of us back in September 2003.

My friend Ernst was 80, and to celebrate his birthday we'd come to Val di Mello to relive memories of visits of long ago. Walled by massive granite slabs, streaked with waterfalls and with a beautiful stream flowing through its meadows, it was difficult to argue with his claim that it's one of the loveliest of all Alpine valleys. He and I had both made several visits in the past, but never together. This would be an opportunity to make amends without any vertical agenda.

He'd booked rooms months in advance at the old hotel at the Bagni del Masino, and as we pulled up outside it had a distinct end-of-season look about it. Steel shutters had been fitted to most of the windows, and in its eyeless state it looked anything but welcoming. The walls were wet from a recent downpour, and the clouds hanging just a few feet above its roof added to the gloom. We were the only guests, and as we ate our first meal that evening in an echoing room whose log fire died through lack of attention, celebration seemed an unlikely prospect.

But Val di Mello did not disappoint. True, we could see no more of its fabled rock walls than their bottom two hundred feet or so, had no view of the waterfalls we could hear thrashing the crags to right and left, and our legs were soaked by the unruly vegetation that overhung the path. Yet the wind-inspired dance of the clouds was magical, and the dripping trees were dressed in early autumn finery unaffected by the weather. Moss-patched boulders added to the enchantment, while the little stone houses and barns that appeared through the mist somehow managed to retain their Italian identity and atmosphere despite the sun's absence. From the mist-shrouded mountains, memories created warmth. Nothing would dampen Ernst's spirits this day. Nor mine.

Discussing summits we could not see, and routes neither of us had climbed nor would ever climb, but recalling those we had seen and tackled on days of blue skies and sunshine kept the magic of that valley alive. Today there were no climbers at work. We had the valley to ourselves. Well, ourselves and the odd farmer tending his cattle on some unseen alp as we slowly wandered beside the stream.

Then we came to a handwritten notice tacked to a wooden post. The letters were blotched with rain, but we could just decipher the message that advertised a *ristorio* open for business. A restaurant? Here? It seemed most unlikely, for all we could see was what appeared to be a rather run-down farm. Ernst grinned, "We'd better check it out."

So we crossed the stream, and as we reached the farmhouse a red-faced woman came across the yard dressed in black tee shirt, jeans, and wellington boots caked with cow dung. In broken Italian, and with tongue in cheek, Ernst enquired whether the restaurant was open, as the notice had suggested. The face broke into an open smile. "Oh si, si," she gushed, wiping her hands on her tee shirt, then patting her long damp hair. "Momento . . . ," and she scurried indoors, emerging a few moments later clutching a pair of large brown mushrooms that she thrust towards us. "Polenta al funghi?"

"That'll do nicely," said Ernst.

The "restaurant" was a trestle table set beneath an overhanging roof extending from a barn. Ernst sat one side, I the other. It would have been pointless to remove our rain gear, for rain was still falling. It ran down the corrugated roof and dripped to the ground just behind me. Should I move, I would be in its direct line of fire. Pools of rainwater stained yellow with dung littered the yard that smelled of cattle and damp hay, and as we drank beer from see-through plastic cups while our meal was being prepared, half a dozen udder-swinging cows wallowed past on their way to the milking parlour, with a black-and-tan dog yapping at their heels.

Neither Ernst nor I had ever been in a restaurant quite like this before.

The woman appeared with our meal. Since we'd last seen her she'd brushed her hair and was now wearing a clean tee shirt. But she'd not changed her jeans or boots, presumably because as soon as we'd finished eating she'd be in the milking parlour with the animals.

She set the food before us, along with odd-sized cutlery wrapped in paper napkins. Then she took a pace backwards, smiling with pride. The steaming *polenta al funghi* filled the plastic plates. Our waitress-cum-chef may not have had the finesse demanded by a top-class restaurant in Milan, but the food certainly looked appetising, and our surprise at finding something to eat at all in such an unexpected location made up for the lack of tablecloth, silver cutlery or a tantalising wine list. Or even walls and a complete roof over our heads.

Polenta may not be the most exciting item on a menu, but lack of choice worked in our favour, for that and the seasoned mushrooms gave us a meal to remember. The ambience of our alfresco dining area was partly responsible for our appreciation. The novelty of finding such a place on a day of damp non-expectation was cause for celebration. The meal went down a treat, and when it was finished I toasted my friend's birthday with another plastic cup of beer.

It was an occasion we would never forget, for it fitted perfectly with the magic of Val di Mello, one of the loveliest of all Alpine valleys. And we wouldn't swap that for any Michelin-starred restaurant.

THE PINK CHÂTEAU

For hundreds of years men have lived among the Alps, and not only in the valleys. Long ago farmers built chalets on the high pastures—the real alps among the Alps—and there they spend the summers grazing their animals and making cheese and butter from their milk. Those chalets have become an important part of the Alpine landscape; they belong. But in 2006, when making yet another tour of Mont Blanc to update my guidebook, I discovered something I considered did not belong. In fact it was an eyesore.

On the eastern side of the Grand Col Ferret, only a few minutes below the pass, a minor trail breaks away from the heavily used route of the Tour of Mont Blanc and leads to a narrow grassy saddle, from which a surprise view is gained along virtually the full length of the Swiss Val Ferret to distant outliers of the Bernese Alps.

Diverting from the main route we cut along the narrow path to capture that view once more, but as the way curved towards the saddle we discovered an old caravan painted a lurid pink that had been placed a few feet from our vantage point. Standing on lumps of breeze block, it was anchored down with guys—no doubt a sensible precaution against being sent flying through the saddle by an Alpine gale to settle in a thousand pieces on some far distant hillside.

But what on earth was a caravan doing here, at 8,200 feet? All around, grass slopes folded away from a rim of frontier peaks. Nearby was some of the most sublime mountain scenery in all Europe—Mont Blanc, Aiguille Noire, Grandes Jorasses, and Mont Dolent. Ahead rose the Grand Combin, beyond which the glorious chain of the Pennine Alps led on and on to the unseen Matterhorn and Monte Rosa.

Yet here stood a caravan; an unsightly *pink* caravan! It was an eyesore, an unwelcome intrusion.

As we stood transfixed by the sight, a man appeared, labouring up the slope with a black-and-white dog which ran towards us, barking. But there was nothing vicious in his bark, and we were unconcerned by it. Neither were we troubled by the new arrival, who simply smiled at us. He carried a long stick, wore a wide-brimmed cowboy hat and had a huge rucksack on his back. Sweat ran in streams down his face and dripped from his chin.

"Bonjour," he panted, taking a key from his pocket. "You like my pink château?"

"This is yours?"

"Only for the summer."

"But what's it doing here—and how did you get it up here?"

He dumped his rucksack, removed the hat, and wiped his brow with his shirt sleeve. "Easy, my friend. It flew 'ere."

"It flew?"

"Of course! It flew—beneath an 'elicopter. A flying château— *my* pink château! You like?" The wide smile, laughing eyes, and obvious eccentricity did little to lessen the impact of this lurid blot on the landscape.

"No," I told him. "I can't say I do."

"Then you 'ave no romance in your soul. And you 'ave no care for the poor shepherd 'oo must spend the summer 'ere looking after a thousand sheep." The grin never shrank, and his eyes continued to flash with humor.

"You're a shepherd?" I asked.

"Of course. 'Ow else could I afford to spend three months in 'eaven? Just me and my dog and a thousand sheep. And my pink château." He gestured at the mountains, the grass slopes, the valley falling away beyond the saddle. "All mine. For three months. Good— yes? Oh, I can see you are jealous! You 'ave just two weeks for 'oliday. Me? I am paid to live 'ere for three months—'eaven! You know?"

His enthusiasm was infectious and we warmed to him, despite his bloody caravan. He explained that he'd never been a shepherd before. He was French, with a home in the Loire valley where he had once studied literature and now worked in a library. He'd seen an advertisement for a shepherd on the internet, thought it would be good to spend a summer alone with his books on a mountainside, had applied for the job and got it. "It's good—yes?"

"I guess it is," I admitted. "But where are your sheep?"

"Oh, over there somewhere," he shrugged, with a nod through the saddle. "I 'ave been away for two days to buy some more food." He tapped the rucksack with his foot, and I heard two bottles rattle against one another. "I will go looking for them tomorrow. I 'ave time," he said. "So 'ave the sheep."

▲

A ROAR OF DISAPPROVAL

Making a solo trek from Chamonix to Zermatt in the summer of 2006 I spent time in the Val d'Hérens checking a couple of remote passes in the ridge behind which lies the Val de Moiry. Those days were extremely warm, and by late afternoon my energy was draining away; I looked forward to nightfall, when the air would be cooler. A bivouac, I figured, would be more appealing than a bed indoors. But I didn't anticipate company.

The prospect of spending yet another night in an airless dormitory was not appealing, so I left Val d'Hérens in the early evening to amble slowly up the hillside in search of a decent bivouac, and by the time I'd passed the last small hamlet hanging from the slope, twilight was sliding towards night. Darkness fell, but my eyes adjusted, and the bare earth path was easy to follow as it angled across the pastures towards a group of trees. On the edge of the woodland a flat stone slab was covered with larch needles. It would make a perfect bed.

Gathering more needles and tufts of pine I created a reasonable mattress and, using the rucksack for a pillow, settled down for the night. A light breeze wafted along the valley, bringing the juicy fragrance of recently cut grass and warm pine. In the distance a river sounded a steady rumble. Stars flashed overhead, a crescent moon was hooked upon a branch, while through the trees the filmy shape of snow mountains disturbed the black spaces.

An hour or so after midnight a sudden roaring, bellowing sound woke me. Heart thrashing, I sat bolt upright, and in the half-darkness I could see the outline of a huge stag with eyes blazing, nostrils flared. The message was clear—I'd invaded his territory.

For a few short moments we stared at one another. Then with another roar of disapproval, he stomped away, pausing now and then to look back and to repeat his complaint.

After that, sleep was a long time coming.

UNEASE ON ICE

Until you become familiar with them and understand their structure, glaciers can seem rather intimidating. As everyone knows, Alpine glaciers are now shrinking fast, thanks to global warming, but they've always contained dangers, such as icefall and crevasse, for anyone straying on them. Where a route crosses a glacier on the way to a mountain hut, in many cases markers are placed to advertise a reasonably safe way. In 1987 Alan Payne and I planned to visit the Mountet hut in the Pennine Alps, which would take us across the Zinal glacier, which seemed straightforward enough.

Ice-crusted peaks at the head of Val de Zinal took on Himalayan proportions as we drew closer to them. Picking our way along the moraine crest 3,000 feet beneath the Bouquetins ridge, it was the Ober Gabelhorn that held our attention, its chiseled summit gleaming above a cascade of ice and snow. Our route to the Mountet hut would pass below it, close to where the Glaciers du Grand Cornier, Durand, and Mountet combine to form the Zinal glacier. It was a direct route marked in summer all the way from where we'd get onto the ice near the end of the moraine.

The moraine crest was narrow and exposed, and in places fixed ropes, chains, and an occasional ladder eased the way where bare slabs and gullies intruded, so when we reached the grassy bluff of the Plan des Lettres, it was so welcoming that we sprawled there in the sunshine for half an hour, simply soaking in the views, content to delay any further activity. But at last, and without a word, Alan stood up, heaved the rucksack onto his shoulders, and began the descent to the glacier. I followed, and a few minutes later we were fitting crampons to our boots and tying on the rope.

We'd crossed plenty of glaciers in the past, Alan and I, both here in the Alps and in the Pyrenees, but there was something different about this one. I felt it the moment we stepped onto ice. Firm and peppered with stones, to all appearances there was little to distinguish it from countless other Alpine glaciers in the summer. Water could be heard gurgling far beneath our boots, while a few narrow streams fled through melted runnels cut in the ice. Where snow still lay, it was either crystallized or slushy; the surface was not flat, but uneven with small mounds here and there. At a glance there was a familiarity about its features, nothing to suggest that it was—well—different. But it was. I couldn't say why or how; I just knew it. And with every step I felt more and more uncomfortable.

I voiced my unease. Alan dismissed it.

But it wouldn't go away. There was something about this glacier, something malevolent. We shouldn't be here, I was sure of that. My stomach churned, my mouth went dry. I strained ears for a warning sound, peered all around me, studied the mountains soaring up on three sides, looking for something that would give a hint of danger. There was none.

But my concern only increased with every step.

"We must turn back," I said.

He gave me a mouthful of abuse without even turning his head, called me a wimp and carried on, several paces ahead, with coils of rope in one hand, ice axe in the other. There was determination in his stride, and I could imagine what he was thinking, for I'd have been the same if our roles had been reversed. But I'd probably call him worse things than a wimp.

Yet I couldn't help it; this sense—no, this *certainty*—that we were in danger of something. But of what I couldn't say.

Tin cans painted red and weighted with stones could be seen weaving a route across the glacier. They were clear to see, easy to follow like waymarks. Crevasses were obvious and narrow enough to step over; the rope was unnecessary. The sun was high and commanding a sky that bore no menace. The few clouds that sailed on a gentle breeze were summer clouds adding character, not threat, their shadows momentarily darkening snowfield and rock face then disappearing without trace. They didn't linger or advertise the approach of a storm.

So why should I feel so uneasy?

No, it had gone beyond unease. Now I was scared.

"Alan, I'm sorry, but we have to get off this bloody glacier—and now! I'm heading back."

And with that I turned around, gave the rope a mighty tug which nearly pulled him off his feet, and almost ran back across the glacier towards the moraine wall, virtually dragging him after me.

By the time we reached the edge of the ice the air was blue with abuse. I'd stretched our years of friendship to the very limit, and he was seething. But as we began to untie the rope that had once united us, a sudden roar caused us to stop and, turning to see what was happening, we watched the central part of the glacier—where we'd been only a few minutes before—collapsing into a large hole that was rapidly spreading outward. All around it the ice was crumbling, folding inward, and tipping into the ever-widening hole. The glacier seemed to be shuddering; at its widest point it had been undercut, and had we not turned back when we did, we'd have been swallowed by it.

There was not a lot to be said then, so we went up to the Plan des Lettres and sat there trembling.

....

The following summer a new route to the Mountet hut was created along the east side of the valley to avoid the Zinal glacier, whose path had now become obsolete due to its dangerous condition.

•   •   •

THE JOY OF DOING NOTHING

Gathering routes for a guidebook meant revisiting districts of the Eastern Alps where I'd walked and climbed in the past, as well as exploring massifs that I knew only by reputation or from a close study of maps. By the summer of 2007 I was close to finalising my selection of regions to include, and spent the first week or so stumbling through atrocious weather. But by the time I'd reached the limestone massifs southeast of Salzburg all that had changed, and the sun rose each morning like a shimmering disc of bronze.

After days of rain and snow summer erupted into furnace-like heat. So my decision to go wandering across the Dachstein was perhaps not the most sensible I'd made so far, for there was little or no shade on its south face when I slid down from the pass and followed a vague trail over slopes of scree that threw back the heat without mercy. I began to regret my choice of route; there was not the slightest breeze, and apart from a pair of chamois and the tiny yellow poppies that somehow managed to cling to life in this inhospitable environment, I had the world to myself. That should have told me something.

Desperate for shade and water to slake my thirst I began to descend. The mountainside was steep, rough and dusty, and I ached from five stifling hours on the go. But at last I came off the rocks and onto the most idyllic of tiny meadows, where a spring fed an infant stream.

The meadow was dotted with boulders and rimmed with larch trees. Flowers starred the grass. Tiny butterflies floated from one delicate flower head to another; insects droned the lazy song of summer. So I dumped my rucksack, drank from the spring, splashed my face, arms and chest, then lay in the shade of a tree and closed my eyes. A tiny songbird piped an aria overhead, while a dull thud told of a larch cone hitting the ground nearby.

As the minutes drifted slowly and multiplied into an hour of lazy contentment, I realized (not for the first time) that sometimes it's not only good, but enriching for the soul, to do nothing. Sometimes it's enough *just to be*. In that lazy hour in an Austrian meadow I was blissfully happy. And knew it.

JUST HANGING AROUND

Often it's where you spend the night, and the people you meet there, that stands out in memory almost as clearly as the journey taken to get there. That was certainly true of one lodging I stayed at in September 1990 on my way from Chamonix to Zermatt.

Hot and weary from a long day's trek across the mountains by way of the Fenêtre d'Arpette, I arrived in Champex in need of a cold drink or two, and somewhere to freshen up and rest my head for the night. The *gîte* at the top end of the main street had all I needed, so I booked in, was allocated a dormitory bed, and within moments was easing aching shoulders under the spray of a powerful shower. What simple pleasure can be gained from just standing beneath a burst of hot, stinging water! All the day's effort, all the aching and sweating, was cleansed from my body, and when I felt sufficiently rejuvenated, I washed my socks too, then stepped out of the shower dressed only in a wet towel.

A Dutchman I'd met the previous evening in Trient emerged from the next cubicle. Similarly clothed in just a wet towel and with his laundered socks in his hand, he asked if I'd seen a drying room. I hadn't, but as a balcony ran outside my dorm I suggested he could hang his wet socks over the rail where I'd be hanging mine. Little did we know the balcony was old and in urgent need of repair.

Padding through the dorm we went out onto the balcony, which overhung the village street, and were just draping our socks over the rail when the timber floor shuddered, creaked, then collapsed into the street, leaving the Dutchman and me hanging from the swaying rail, dressed only in wet towels and wondering how we were going to get out of our predicament.

Suddenly there came a cry from the street below. It was a German trekker who'd also been in Trient the previous night.

"Hold it there," he called, waving his camera. "I would like a photo of this."

WALKING ON ICE

There are days in the mountains when it's imperative to keep moving—to stay ahead of a storm, for example, or to complete a route in safety before darkness falls. There are also times when you seem to have an excess of energy, or when adrenalin promotes a feeling of invincibility and you fill every moment with activity. But sometimes—and they could be the best—you arrive at a place which seems so perfect that you put all carefully laid plans to one side, stop where you are, and simply absorb the beauty that surrounds you. Making a crossing of the Petersgrat in 1989 was one such occasion.

Near the head of the Gasterntal an old Englishman supported the weight of his body on a stick while his chest heaved up and down. "You okay?" I asked. He nodded, for he had no breath with which to speak. But he didn't appear to be in distress, just weary, standing there on the path all alone, slightly hunched, with beads of sweat on his brow and a watery gleam in his eye. He wore a cloth cap, a jacket, and neat shirt and tie, climbing breeches from the 1950s, and long blue patterned socks. His heavy leather boots had been polished as new. On his back hung an ancient A-framed rucksack, with practically nothing in it.

"Just drawing breath," he said at last. "That's all." Then added, "A grand valley, this," indicating back the way we'd come. Down there beyond a wonderland of rock gardens, tiny goats could be seen grazing near the farm of Heimritz. We could see the track that had brought us from Selden, but not the lovely old inn itself, for that was hidden by trees. Further on, the valley was walled by the Balmhorn, and just this side of it lay the Lötschenpass. That view held plenty of memories, and not just for the old man. The Gasterntal was a long-time favorite of mine too.

"It certainly is," I agreed.

A dreamy glaze came over the old man's eye. "Happy days," he said. "Yes, happy days . . . D'you know, this is my first summer since the war without an ice axe? The guides won't take me now; they think I'll die on some remote peak. Ha! That would be the way to go, don't you think?"

We left him standing there with his memories and continued along the path towards ice cliffs at the foot of the Kanderfirn. Projecting over a band of rocks, they were a luminous blue where outer chunks had broken away, exposing a fresh, clean underbelly of ice whose melt darkened the rocks.

"I'm eighty-two," the old man called after us. "Eighty-two, but I'm still game."

The trail climbed steeper now, with zigzags taking us over a bluff, then it eased along a grit-strewn ledge beside the glacier. We roped up, but didn't bother with crampons as the glacier had a good covering of snow.

Ascent of the Kanderfirn was straightforward, like walking up a long, easy angled ramp. There were few crevasses, visibility was good, and we were in no rush. We could enjoy the day without pressure, which suited Roland, who'd managed to persuade his boss to give him two days off from his job as a chef at a hotel on the banks of the Thunersee, so our planned crossing of the Petersgrat could be taken at a leisurely pace. We'd known each other for twenty-odd years, Roland and I, and whenever I found myself near where he was working at the time, we'd try to snatch a day or two together for a climb or a pass crossing. He'd worked in so many different regions of the Swiss Alps that he'd gathered an almost encyclopaedic knowledge of them. But between seasons he'd go traveling for a month or two, sending letters from distant lands full of lively tales. Despite English not being his first language, he had a way of describing landscape and people that I, as a writer, envied.

We spent the night at the Mutthorn hut. It was like being on an island of rock in a sea of ice, for glaciers spilled away in almost every direction. Despite being mid-July, the hut was almost empty and the dormitory cold. Since I'd left my sleeping bag down in the valley, I spent the night in a foetal position wrapped in three blankets, and in the morning rose with a stiff neck, anxious to get some exercise.

The early light stained the snow and ice outside the hut as the sun rose far off. The sky was clear; it would be another good day. We looked down into the head of the Lauterbrunnen valley and out to the Faulhorn, but from above the hut the Eiger appeared, and seen side-on it had the sharpness of a spear. The Jungfrau was unrecognisable from here, having lost the elegant purity that makes it such an icon of the Oberland. From above the Mutthorn hut it was almost dull. Big, yes, but without its clean white veil it had lost something special.

The Petersgrat was only 650 feet above the hut, and we were there in no time, crunching our way along the remnant of that vast sheet of ice that once covered much of the Bernese Alps. Ice crystals danced in the sunlight, and whichever way we turned mountains crowded every horizon. I thought of the old Englishman and imagined him standing there with us. No doubt he would have given a potted history of every peak and reminisced about their summits. Perhaps we should have invited him to join us.

Directly opposite where we stood, the Bietschhorn revealed its pyramid of rock and ice, while all the southern view contained the range of the Pennine Alps, stretching from the Dom to Mont Blanc. The Lötschental lay far below, nearly 4,500 feet below the great white ridge on which we stood; we could not see into it, but then we were content with the world as it appeared from here. The Lötschental could wait.

For now we were happy to forget our plans.

Without discussion we dumped our rucksacks and sat on them. Roland lit his pipe, and for a whole hour we had no need for words. The sun rose higher, the air warmed; I removed my down jacket, applied more suncream. And dreamed into the view.

Yes, the Lötschental could wait. This was a time and a place to savor.

ONE SUNSET TOO MANY

In May 1998 I was sent to Austria by a travel company to check routes for a small walking guide. Despite my arguing that it was too early in the season, and that any worthwhile ridge walks and other trails on the upper slopes were likely still to be under snow, they were convinced that conditions would be fine and I'd find enough to satisfy their clientele. They were wrong, and from the very start it looked as though I'd be wasting my time, but after descending from white-out conditions to a village in the valley, the day took an unexpected turn.

"I see you are an artist." The woman's voice surprised me, for I was completely unaware of her arrival in the damp village square where I'd been seated for half an hour feeding the sparrows, then focusing my camera on them as they perched on the iron spout of a water fountain. Until an hour ago I was on the mountain above the village, but deep snow and an almost total lack of visibility had driven me down. Having used my compass from the moment I'd left the first cable car of the season, I'd been forced to admit that my prediction had been correct—that summer was still some weeks off, and it was too early to have any chance of getting the photos and route information required. In frustration I'd given up, plunged down into the valley where it was merely raining, and was now wondering how to fill the rest of the day.

"I have been watching you from my room," the woman confessed with the husky voice of a heavy smoker. "I too am an artist, a painter, and would like you to see my work." At least, that's what I interpreted her guttural German to mean.

Beneath the colored golf umbrella I could just make out a halo of salt-and-pepper hair in need of a good brush. Large hoop-like rings dangled from her ears, reminding me of a fairground fortune teller. She had painted eyebrows and a wide mouth enlarged even more by bright red lipstick; a mauve patch of a birthmark spread over her cheek beneath one eye. She wore a loose waterproof jacket, a faded cotton dress, wellington boots, and a cluster of rings on several nicotine-stained fingers. Flamboyant, I guess, would be one way to describe her.

"I'm no artist," I argued. "Just taking photos, that's all."

"Ah, you are English!" Immediately she switched to my own language, spoken with flair and a lot of activity with her free hand.

"I once had a loverrr from St Ives," she explained, rolling the "r" in lover. "We lived among artists, the sea was good, but it was not the mountains; so after several years I left them and came home. I haf to paint mountains, you see; they are my inspiration, my reason for liffing. You will understand that, for although you say you are not an artist, I think you are modest." With a theatrical pose and a tilt of her head she continued: "I can recognize a true artist when I see one. We are two of a kind. And you must see my work. I insist." She reached out a hand and gestured that I should follow. So with no other plans to fill the afternoon, I followed. At the very least I'd be out of the rain.

Her house was at the far end of the square, where the old wooden door had been left ajar. She pushed it open and, stepping inside, shook the umbrella, and kicked off her boots. She left them where they lay, dropped the umbrella beside them, then twirled around barefooted to face me. "Look," she gestured at the hallway walls that were covered in paintings. "I haf to paint mountains."

Despite what she said, I'm no artist. I can tell a Picasso from a Rembrandt, but consider a lot of modern art to be the emperor's new clothes, for where artistic talent exists I imagine it should be recognisable. And I didn't see much evidence of it here. Well meant, and created in a fury of passion, identical globules of paint were smeared and spattered over canvas after canvas. The colors were lurid, and at first I had no idea what they could possibly represent.

"I will show you more, then we will drink a coffee and discuss."

I bent down to remove my boots. "Leaf them, leaf them," she insisted. But I removed them anyway and traipsed after her along the hallway, leaving a trail of damp footprints on the floor. My socks were wet from melted snow.

At the end of the hall she pushed open another door. "My studio," she proudly announced.

It was a mess, smelling of cigarette smoke, oil paint, and turpentine, with tatty rags and old strips of newspaper strewn across the floor. On a small table an open wooden box contained assorted brushes and well-squeezed tubes of paint; a smock lay crumpled beside it, and an empty cigarette packet yawned from a wicker chair.

There were windows on two sides. One looked onto a narrow street; the other gave a view across meadows to a distant wall of mountains misted by the steady drizzle. Those mountains were the Steinernes Meer—the limestone massif known as the Sea of Stones that carries the border dividing Austria from Bavaria. I'd wandered across their southern flank many years ago and recalled the alpine plants that flowered in the crevices of bone-white slabs.

How different those mountains appeared today spattered with snow and seen through a watery veil.

"You see now," she said, lighting a cigarette and drawing the smoke deep into her lungs, "this is my reason for liffing." But when I turned to her, she was not looking out of the window, but at her latest work on an easel. A few brushstrokes only had been applied as an outline of the scene that would no doubt soon erupt in more splodges. But at least this work in progress had shape and a hint of reality, and as such I recognized the mountains seen from her window. What she was depicting was the Steinernes Meer. Over and over and over again.

A blue-tiled stove took up a good part of the wall opposite the window with a view, and above it hung one of the woman's large paintings in a home-made frame. Now seen from a few paces distant, I could appreciate its resemblance to the frontier mountains, the garish colors announcing a sunset sky, with shadows and a stain of alpenglow washing across the steep crags. There was no detail, but none should be expected, for when seen from the vantage point of her house, the mountains appeared as a single, unified, featureless block. The painting reflected that; it was, if nothing else, impressionistic, and suddenly the canvas came alive. The fact that the mountains, seen from this angle, would never have the sun setting behind them mattered not at all. This was how she imagined it, how she wished it to be. Artistic licence was her pre-rogative. Who was I to judge?

"I work here all the year," she explained. "Sometimes outside, and in the winter it can be very cold, but when I work I do not notice. Only when I stop do my hands ache. When I work my blood is hot. It is the passion. Come, there is more to see."

She took me into another room—this one with worn furniture, and art magazines scattered everywhere as though a window had been left open and a gale had swept through. Two ash trays needed emptying. And on the walls were yet more near-identical paintings. Each one depicted the Steinernes Meer at sunset. Large or small, both the subject and interpretation were the same, all expressed in a riot of color. Sometimes the emphasis was blue; sometimes she'd been heavy with sienna; in one the sunset was almost green. But in an alcove with poor lighting hung the por-trait of an old woman slumped in a chair. It was either not very good or the old woman was a freak of nature and the chair that supported her had been made by someone with no sense of scale. There was also a vase of flowers with a nudge towards Van Gogh on one of his off-days.

I understood then why she concentrated on mountains.

"To the kitchen," she cried, and taking me by the sleeve pulled me back along the hallway and through a door on the left. House-work was clearly not a priority, and while she searched for a cup that did not contain the remains of last week's coffee, I glanced above the mayhem to walls virtually hidden by paintings I no longer had difficulty in recognising. The Steinernes Meer at sunset, half a dozen times.

"We drink a coffee," she insisted. "Then you tell me what you think."

At that my heart sunk. What could I honestly say about one sunset too many?

HENRY V GOES WALKABOUT

Throughout the year I receive a steady stream of letters and emails from strangers happy to share their experience of following routes described in my guidebooks. Some point out mistakes, offer suggestions or give information about changes that have occurred since the book went to print. Each one is gratefully received, for such feedback helps to improve future editions and, at the same time, creates a relationship between author and reader—readers who become valued friends without faces, most of whom will never be met in person. But in 2006 we were hiking around the Tour of Mont Blanc, checking details for a new edition of the guidebook, when the need for anonymity became apparent.

I once spent two happy hours with a couple of trekkers in a hut in the Swiss Alps, but their attitude changed the moment the hut keeper let slip that the person who had written their guidebook was sharing their table. From then on I was treated like a Westminster champion, with the indignity of being "surreptitiously" photographed from just about every angle and in every activity. Well, almost every activity.

So I guard anonymity whenever I'm following routes for which I've produced guidebooks. After all, who would want to be confronted by an irate reader who was "lost" only yesterday through something you'd written?

So there we were, blithely trekking around the Tour of Mont Blanc, checking details for a new edition of the guide, and chatting happily with other walkers met on the trail, or in huts and hotels, without fear of recognition. Introductions were neither expected nor necessary; we were all bound upon the same course. Equals on the trail, we shared a common experience and expressed similar delight with scenes that caught our breath, whether for the first or the nth time of seeing.

When we reached Rifugio Bonatti, that splendid modern hut above the Italian Val Ferret with its direct view of the south side of the Grandes Jorasses, the *gardien* allocated a long table specifically for English-speaking guests, and when dinner was called we discovered no less than six copies of my TMB guide spread among the other diners—and it was the main topic of conversation . . . Min and I avoided eye contact throughout the meal and made a few murmured comments only when the conversation required. We became "the quiet couple" who made an early exit, explaining we were tired and needed to get our heads down.

Two days later we had crossed the Grand Col Ferret, spent a night in a *gîte* where we were the only Brits, and wandered through a meadow in the Swiss Val Ferret. When we stopped to change a film in my camera, along came Peter, the man who had sat next to me at dinner that evening in the Bonatti refuge. After exchanging a few pleasantries, he suddenly asked, "Do you know Shakespeare's Henry V?"

I told him I did.

"Do you remember the scene when, on the night before Agincourt, Henry walks around his camp in disguise, listening to what his troops were saying about him?"

"Er, yes."

"Well, you're Henry V," he said, and strode away with a grin.

▲

HEART OF THE STORM

An act of serendipity led to my spending much of the summer of 1994 among the Eastern Alps, beginning in the far west of Austria

and heading eastward from one massif to the next with a free travel
pass in my pocket, boots on feet, rucksack on back and, for much of
the time, sunshine on my shoulder.

Nostalgia brought me back to the village by the lake. Almost thirty years ago, in the last summer of innocence before getting married, I'd had a base there from which I led mountain holidays. Once a fortnight I'd take a day off and would often use it to make a solo trek round a fine horseshoe of peaks, starting shortly after daybreak and returning to base about ten hours later—hungry, weary, sun-baked, but content.

Now I was back in the district to work on a brochure for the Austrian National Tourist Office, and that horseshoe of peaks rising from the opposite shore appeared too tempting to ignore. With a day in hand I figured it would be good to hike that circuit once more and recapture views that had never been quite forgotten, despite eclipse by hundreds—maybe thousands—of others, every one of which had been memorable but different. I wouldn't bother to buy a map—having followed that route several times in the past, I'd surely remember the way once I got started. Or so I thought.

So I took the ferry, strode up a narrow lane, and found the start of the old, familiar trail by a balconied farm almost strangled by petunias. It led into a meadow that was shadeless, July-sticky, the air moist enough to wring out—like the kitchen walls that would run with soapy water on washday when I was a lad. Today it was my face that ran, not with soapy water but with sweat, as the trail now seemed a lot steeper than I remembered. When last there all those years ago I carried only the very basic essentials; now I was burdened by a rucksack filled with the needs of a five-week tour. And my legs were nearly thirty years older than they had been then.

I began to feel my age.

A patch of woodland gave shade, but denied access to any breath of air. I drew deeply on the scent of warm pine as a red squirrel that was almost black chased along the path with a zigzag bounding gait, then shot straight up a tree without slackening pace. I envied its agility, then stepped out into the full glare of summer once more.

The trail went up. And up. There were more meadows dotted with barns, eye-stingingly sharp with the fragrance of freshly cut hay. Snug in those meadows gray boulders were patched with lichen, the grass having been scythed right to their edges. Nothing was left to waste. Butterflies searched for flowers as grasshoppers leapt away from my boots. Distant mountains grew fuzzy with heat haze. I dripped.

As I worked my way higher, so the lake in the valley shrank to the size of a paddling pool. The summit of my first peak still seemed a long way off as memory showed signs of betrayal. I used to romp up this slope, along the ridge, onto the summit, a quick drink at the hut, then off along the continuing ridge to the next summit, then the next . . . Or so I recalled. What I didn't remember were the trees on the lower part of the first ridge. Surely that used to be bare rock? I noticed individual features that played no part in that long-gone history. Was the hut still there? Was the hut on this peak—or the next?

It was all speculation as I had no map.

My rests were becoming more frequent for I was growing tired, yet I was still a fair distance from the first peak when I noticed an evil scum of cloud advancing my way. Sunlight broke into the cloud and was consumed by it. The heat became oppressive, and I grew anxious with the certainty that a storm was brewing. My hope now was to reach the hut on the summit before it arrived. To get there involved climbing the ridge, and ridges are places to avoid in a storm. I'm not a gambler, but on this occasion I gambled on having sufficient speed and energy to make it in time.

I didn't.

The storm broke, catching me on the ridge with at least 300 feet left to climb. So I slithered off it and lost as much height as I could as fast as I could; height that had cost a lot of effort to gain. All around me the air seemed charged with electricity; my heart was racing, my nerves were raw, no doubt my hair was standing upright—but I couldn't see that. There was nowhere to hide and I could not outrun the inevitable, so I threw down my rucksack, knelt on it, and with head down submitted to the onslaught.

Vivid blue-white eruptions of lightning seethed and sparked the mountain's ridge where I'd been moments before; thunder was instantaneous, deafening, scary. It crackled like artillery fire, then ripped the heavens apart. An unfamiliar smell accompanied it. Cordite—could that be it? Another blinding flash, and an explosion that set my ears ringing. The temperature plummeted, and at first rain, then large pieces of hail, stung my flesh through protective clothing. A wind came from nowhere to thrash me; the mountain shook and I trembled like a child. This was the closest I'd ever been to the heart of a storm, and here in the open, as flash succeeded flash, I was fully aware of what could happen. I confess that I was terrified.

Then suddenly and without reason I experienced a great sense of calm. Fear evaporated. I opened my eyes, raised my head and looked into the vortex, the madness of swirling ice particles and forbidding tatters of cloud. The air was violent around me, yet I was bewitched by the beauty of nature in her most savage mood. She was angry, vengeful, full of spite. She was wild, restless, and beyond man's taming. I was vulnerable and at her mercy, and knew it. Yet I saw the moment as a gift and felt a surge of happiness as I sought to capture an experience I may never have again. I swear I smiled, not as a challenge to nature's supremacy, but out of respect. It was the smile of awe and admiration.

All of life is experience, and sometimes it's the things we fear more than anything that grant the most telling lessons. But you have to survive them to know it.

RÄTIKON PARADISE

Limestone ranges are especially rich in alpine flowers, and wandering among them in early summer can be an unforgettable experience. In July 2010 I was researching routes for yet another guide. From the very start flowers had been such a feature that the time taken to hike from one hut to the next was often extended by the need to identify and photograph countless different species. Sometimes the sheer abundance of flowers was almost beyond comprehension. Often it was fragrance that caught the attention first; day by day we were romanced by nature's bounty.

For two weeks we'd made our journey along and across the Silvretta and Rätikon Alps, weaving a route from Switzerland to Austria and back again, linking valleys by way of a variety of cols, mostly rocky and remote, some leading onto glaciers that had shrunk considerably in the seven years since I'd last been there (descent on near-vertical scree to reach them had led to some heart-in-mouth moments). We'd slept in huts and dreamed by streams, been dazzled by meadows so full of flowers there was no room for a blade of grass to intrude, and enjoyed the contrasts of crystalline rocks of the Silvretta and the Rätikon's shattered limestone. We'd been soaked through once or twice and wearied by the heat, but we could celebrate the best of mountain days in a harmony of trust and understanding. It had been a journey of smiles.

Now Min and I were alone. Our friends had left for home this morning; we'd watched them descend the slope below the Schesaplana hut, and as they grew smaller we gathered our rucksacks and took to the eastbound trail that would entice us back along the flank of the mountain, up to the Cavelljoch and across the

Kirchlispitzen screes, on to the Drusenfluh, and eventually to the sturdy Carschina hut to spend a last night under the battlements of the Sulzfluh. Just the two of us, stepping into wonderland.

I'd walked this trail before, several years ago, but I was alone then and traveled in the opposite direction. I remembered sunlight glancing off bleached stone—a maze of limestone pinnacles, boulders, and fingers of rock that had once belonged to the Drusenfluh's broken south face. I recalled how I'd been stopped in my tracks time and again by a cascade of flowers and wondered how they could possibly survive (and in such quantities) in what was, to all appearances, a savage and hostile environment. Here nature rose to every challenge and displayed a power beyond my understanding. Flowers; everywhere there had been alpine flowers, and I'd been bewitched by them.

Now I was back and, squeezing one last day from our two-week allowance, was anxious to relive and share those long-cherished places with my wife. There were no disappointments, for we stepped from one extravagant rock garden to the next. Great clusters of alpenrose splashed the hillsides with pink and blood red, offset by the rich greenery of their leaves and a scattering of white stone. Trumpet gentians of vivid blue, cushions of androsace and saxifrage, and two-colored violas filtered onto the actual pathway. It was difficult to remain true to our route, for diversions called in every direction. And so we strayed.

In the midst of the most perfect of natural gardens we sat to chew on a piece of dry bread and the remains of our cheese, choosing a place among low pock-marked rocks in whose hollows houseleek rosettes had found anchorage and now projected thick succulent stems that ended with crimson stars. A drift of tiny daphne flowers spilled out from beneath the rocks, their delicate pink florets sending up a generous waft of perfume. The air was rich with its fragrance, and we grew heady with its seduction.

It was then that Min spoke, softly and with a quiver of emotion. "If I should die tomorrow," she said, "know that I've already been to Paradise."

BREAKFAST ON A TRAY

Travels among the Eastern Alps in the summer of 1994 brought me to the Salzkammergut region, a popular district of lakes and mountains where I planned to spend a few days with notebook and camera. Being alone, I gave little advanced thought to where I'd stay, but was prepared to take whatever was available—which was just as well, as it turned out.

Bad Ischl was full when I arrived. Every hotel and *gasthof* had been booked in advance; there were no beds left.

"It is the high season," the woman at the tourist office explained with a sigh that suggested I was a fool not to realize it. But I was content to take pot luck, and if there was nowhere to stay, I'd find a meadow and sleep beneath the stars. I didn't tell her that, of course, but smiled and said, "Okay. Thanks anyway," and bent down for my rucksack and prepared to leave.

As I did she turned to a colleague, then called me back. "There is just one possibility. Not a hotel, not even a *gasthof*, but a room only. *Perhaps* a room," she emphasized. "Just outside town. Only a room you understand, no meals. You like for me to try?"

She opened a drawer in her desk, pulled out a notebook, flicked through some pages, found a number, reached for the telephone. A full minute passed before a voice answered, and I spent that minute looking out at the mountains of Salzkammergut I intended to explore in the coming days. This was Austria's lake district, and I needed to get some photos—not only of the mountains and lakes, but of some of its villages too. Bad Ischl had seemed an obvious base, and if it meant sleeping in a meadow out of sight, I'd deal with that. Now it seemed a bivouac might not be necessary.

Twenty minutes later I was studying the town map given to me at the tourist office, checking the name of a nondescript back street against an address on the paper in my hand, then searching for the grocery indicated by a cross. I found it wedged between tall buildings, separated from one by a narrow alley. Inside the shop I had to take care not to demolish the stock with my rucksack while I asked the young woman behind the counter where I could find the lady whose name was scribbled on the back of my map—a name which was quite incomprehensible to me.

"Come this way," she beckoned to a doorway concealed by long strings of colored beads that hooked on my glasses as I squeezed through. The doorway led into the alley, which opened onto a paved courtyard surrounded by buildings. Cardboard boxes and a mess of old vegetables spilled onto the ground, drawing the attention of a scrawny tortoiseshell cat. The cat eyed me with disdain, turned a lip, then scampered down the alleyway.

The young woman from the grocery pointed to a window on the first floor of one of the buildings. She called a name. Once, twice, three times. A curtain moved, half a face peered down at us, and a hand twitched.

The young woman pushed open a door. "Go up," she said. "First floor. You will see."

The stairs were uncarpeted. Four were of stone, the rest wood, but the first-floor landing had a worn strip of oilcloth down the center. It led to a door that stood ajar. "Come in," whispered a voice.

In a dark and cluttered room a woman in her seventies sat hunched over a table, from which papers cascaded onto the carpet. "Are you the English?" Her voice was soft and frail. It matched her features—the parchment face whose complexion was exaggerated by the severe black shawl and skirt and starched white blouse she wore. Her steel-gray hair was pulled tight into a bun, so tight that her otherwise wrinkled skin was stretched smooth towards her ears.

"You need a room," she told me. It was not a question, and without waiting for my response she took a key from the table and handed it to me. "At the top." She pointed to the ceiling. "It's all there is. Toilet on the landing. No-one else. If you want breakfast it will be outside your room at eight o'clock. First you go and see."

"No, I'm sure it's fine," I said. "I'll take it."

I was surprised then at the tone of her voice when she answered. It was suddenly firm and strong, a voice that would allow no discussion. "No! You will go see first. Then you will tell me. If you agree, we make contract."

The building was four stories high and every stair creaked; each one had its own special sound. Had I been agile enough I could have played a tune by running from one to another. But I'm not, so I creaked my way to the top of the building, noted the makeshift wooden cubicle that housed the toilet on the landing, and opened the door to my room.

It was hot and airless under the roof, and when I pushed open the skylight, even more hot air fell in. I wouldn't need a duvet tonight.

There was nothing fancy about this room—a faded religious picture on a bare wall, a cheap put-you-up bed whose springs sagged, a ceramic wash basin with a tap that coughed rust-colored water, a small wooden table with one leg propped up on a beer mat, and two simple chairs, both of which would benefit from some glue. And that was it.

I stood my rucksack against the bed and descended three flights of stairs. The old lady knew I was coming. No doubt the young woman in the shop across the way did too. Those stairs were really noisy.

"Well? I told you that's all there is." Her tone was dismissive.

"It's good enough for me," I told her. "Three nights okay?"

She looked surprised at that, and her voice softened. It was almost friendly now. "If you like. Three nights—or more."

"Three should be enough. Thanks."

Among the papers on her table she had an official-looking pad on which she wrote her name and address, then pushed it to me to do likewise. Name, age, nationality, form of employment, address, passport number, method of travel, date of arrival, date of departure. Signature. She switched on a table lamp and studied what I had written, and while she did this my attention was drawn to a framed photograph standing like an island amid a sea of papers. The woman in the photograph was clearly the old lady, but when she was much, much younger. She looked less severe then; attractive with a warm smile, a Sunday-best hat perched upon a toss of fair hair, a simple patterned dress that reached just below her knees, smart shoes, a handbag down by her side, her left arm round the shoulders of a boy whose hair had been slicked down especially for the photographer.

"Is this your son?" I asked in innocence, and was completely unprepared for the response, for she lifted the photo to her cheek, kissed it, snuffled, choked, then tears poured down her face as she folded in grief.

I didn't know what to say. Should I attempt to comfort her? Or softly tiptoe away?

Her shoulders rose and fell as she gulped back the tears, and without releasing the photograph, she leaned across to an old writing desk half-buried by books, opened a drawer and held out a newspaper cutting for me to read.

My German is poor, but it was clear that what she had given me was the formal announcement of her son's death two months ago. The face of a man in his forties stared out at me, his name printed in bold letters beneath. The face was an older version of the boy in the tear-stained photograph held against his mother's face. "My son Franz," she gulped. "My angel. My only dear son."

I didn't sleep too well that night. Twice I got out of bed and stood on one of the chairs with my head out of the skylight hoping for a breeze off the mountains. None came, and when I did drift off, it was to dream of a young mother and her son dancing across a meadow with arms outstretched like Julie Andrews in The Sound of Music.

In the morning, shortly before eight, I crossed the landing to the toilet, and when I returned to my room I found a tray outside the door, with a flask of coffee, a cup and saucer, a small jug of milk, four sugar cubes, two thick slices of bread on a plate, a knob of butter and strawberry jam in a dish.

How had it arrived? I swear it wasn't there when I went to the toilet only moments before, and I hadn't heard anyone coming up the stairs—or descending them. It was impossible to step on those stairs, or the landing, without the boards creaking loud enough to be heard outside in the street. Impossible. I'd tried it and failed.

Yet here was my breakfast, and it could only have arrived by way of the stairs!

Bewildered by an inability to explain its appearance, I carried the tray into my room, set it upon the table, and ate.

The following morning I looked out of my room a few minutes before eight o'clock. No breakfast tray, so I studied the route I'd chosen for the day on my map spread across the bed, and when I checked again, my breakfast had arrived. Once again I'd not heard any feet on the stairs. How could that be? I was intrigued, so decided I would be extra alert on my third and final morning.

I was. Or at least, I thought I was.

At 7:55 the landing was deserted. At 7:56 I opened my bedroom door a few inches and sat with a full view of the stairs. I strained my ears; the old building was silent. Nothing stirred.

The minutes crept towards eight o'clock. I heard a clock chime. No breakfast. At five minutes past eight, still no breakfast. I was thirsty, but I'd just filled my water bottle with iced tea bought yesterday in the grocery nearby. It stood upon the table just two paces from my chair. I stood up, reached for it, and knocked it over. The Sigg bottle fell with a crash to the floor, and when I'dpicked it up and turned around, I smelled fresh coffee and caught sight of the corner of a breakfast tray just outside my half-opened door . . .

UNDER LEADEN SKIES

Many will remember 1999 as the year of the total eclipse of the sun. Not I. That year I was concentrating on the mountains and valleys of the Massif des Écrins. It was an undeniably challenging summer and a truly memorable one — but not for reasons I'd anticipated. As for the eclipse, such was the density of cloud cover that it passed without my noticing.

The summer spent researching a guide to the Écrins National Park was the wettest I'd ever known. The flysheet of my fifteen-year-old tent leaked during the very first night, and before long my sleeping bag was damp throughout. By the third evening I had to drape overtrousers and waterproof jacket over the inner tent beneath the leaks to deflect the steady trickle of water seeping through the fly. I'd cook in the porch with stove and utensils resting in a pool, while the familiar crackling thunder of another approaching storm became the summer's soundtrack.

But I would set out each morning regardless, and at some time during the day there'd usually be a break in the clouds—the rain would cease and a beam or two of sunlight would burst through, choose a peak, ridge or rock face to illuminate, and give an uplift of spirits before being banished by the next racing cloud stream. Yet leaden skies failed to deny the mountains their grandeur.

When I'd exhausted the possibilities of one valley, I'd collapse the tent, strap it to the top of my rucksack, cross the mountains into the next valley, and seek out the driest possible site on which to settle while I explored for another week or so. That way my knowledge of the district steadily grew; the names of villages, alps, glaciers and snowfields, huts, peaks, and passes emerged from a soggy map into recognisable features. And a love of the Écrins blossomed despite the daily storms.

In the very heart of the massif the tiny mountaineers' village of La Bérarde was my final port of call. I should have known better. Nestling at the head of the Vallée du Vénéon at the confluence of two mountain torrents below the Barre des Écrins, the village camp-site seemed vulnerable, for the rumble and crunch of rocks being shifted in the stream bed was a potent reminder of the weeks of bad weather. Yet I chose to ignore it—the eternal optimist, I looked on the sunshine that welcomed me as a sign that an Indian summer was about to take over. Lazing on the summit of the Tête de la Maye 2,500 feet above the tent reinforced that optimism, and with the highest of French mountains outside the Mont Blanc massif demanding attention, I could forget the frustrating calendar of views denied thus far. This, surely, made all the wet weeks worthwhile.

The following day challenged that optimism. There were no views, as the valleys once again were swamped with bruise-colored clouds. Lightning sizzled, the mountains reverberated with thunder, and a tide of freezing rain was thrown by the wind. Up at the Temple Écrins refuge I tried to warm cold fingers with a mug of coffee as hailstones bounced off the roof, and when there was a brief respite I ran back down to the valley, turned left, and headed for the Refuge de la Pilatte, noted for the cascading glacier behind it and Les Bans that towers high above. I saw neither, and the brightest moment of the day was when I crawled into my tent several hours later to discover no more than two new pools of water had formed on my sleeping mat.

I'd just finished eating when a helicopter could be heard flying low over the campsite. Back and forth it went, momentarily drowning out the angry sounds of the river and the steady beat of rain on wet tent. Then it flew away and darkness fell.

Suddenly a shout woke me. Instructions to evacuate were deciphered. "Take just your valuables and go," was the gist of it. "Leave your tent and assemble at the CAF building. Now!"

Passport, money and sleeping bag were thrust into my rucksack. Pulling on rain gear and boots I erupted from the tent into the fury of the latest storm. Headlamp beams were all aiming for the footbridge giving access to the village, and as I stepped onto the bridge I could feel it moving under the strain of the brown flood of water, the crash of rocks against wooden piles advertising its weakness. Then above the shrieking storm and surging river the louder and more fearful sound of rockfall told of mountains loosening under the onslaught of so much rain.

That night I slept on the floor of a large public room alongside thirty other refugees from the storm, and in the morning, with the weather now full of contrition and a weak beam of sunlight seeking forgiveness, I returned to the campsite where my tent sat alone on an island mound—soggy and sagging, but still intact. It was time to go exploring again.

FOR THE THANK YOU

For two glorious summers I guided walking holidays based in Italy's Val Gardena, each day wandering some of the most visually exciting trails in the Dolomites. Some snaked between slender towers, a few crossed meadows of flower and ribbed rock, while others teetered along ridges or angled across screes. There were no dull moments, for the sheer variety of opportunities was such that a lifetime would be insufficient to do justice to them all. One typically bright summer's morning in 2003, my plan was to take a route I'd followed only once before, but which I felt sure my group would enjoy.

Our day began with views of the Sassolungo at the head of the valley and the massive block of the Sella massif on the far side of Passo Gardena. It progressed among a labyrinth of bizarre fingers and seemingly fragile pinnacles of rock on the climb to Passo Cir, had rewarded with a generous vista from Passo Crespëina, and heralded promise for more good things in the coming hours. The Dolomites, with all their exotic masonry, their alpine flowers, dwarf pines, upstanding coral reefs, debris-strewn *altipianos* and ever-changing light patterns, were at their extravagant best, and my group responded well—as they had each and every day. As they should.

We'd stopped for a breather a little short of the narrow and exposed rib of the Forcella de Ciampac, which was just out of sight, when a woman approached. She was white-faced and trembling, and when our eyes met I could see she was near to tears.

Standing before me, and noting my group looking relaxed and at ease, she stuttered something in German about the way being no good, too much broken, steep, a fall. A fall? Her words were confused and confusing. Flustered, she gestured back the way she'd come, said something about her husband and friends having gone ahead to the *rifugio*. She would meet them there, but the way—"no good, too much broken, fall, falling." Or something like that. A tear rolled down her cheek. She snuffled and blew her nose.

Fearing an accident I stood up and, telling the group to wait while I checked the situation, I then turned to the woman. "Show me," I said.

She pointed along the trail and shuffled slowly behind me, but when I reached the *forcella* and peered over the edge where the mountainside swept down towards the Vallunga, there was nothing to raise any concern. I looked the other side; another slope, steeper than the first, but no sign of an accident there either. Ahead? Nothing.

Then I understood. There had been no accident. It was the path itself that caused her distress; she was suffering an attack of vertigo.

I smiled and held out my hand. "Come," I told her quietly. "I will help you across."

She gave me both her trekking poles and clutched my hand, very tightly. She was trembling again, her palm was clammy, her tears were real. Then with slow but determined steps we made our way across the slender rib of rock where the view was dramatic on both sides, birds circling below, their cries echoing against the crags. I looked over my shoulder and noted that her eyes were almost closed, shutting out as best she could the big drops to right and left. And in moments we were across, the problem was over.

Now her face spread into the widest of smiles. "Danke!" she gasped, "Grazie mille! Thank you!" With obvious relief she took her sticks from me and scampered off along the trail that rose into a gully ahead. I went back to my group.

An hour later we were sitting outside Rifugio Puez, with its view down the length of Vallunga, whose vertical cliffs funnelled attention towards the distant Val Gardena, when the German woman approached our table. With bright eyes that showed no sign of her earlier distress, she handed me a glass of schnapps. "It is for the thank you," she said, and several tables away, the man I took to be her husband raised a glass and nodded.

RECORDING HISTORIC LANDSCAPES

The Alps are falling apart. Those apparently solid blocks of ancient masonry are fragile; the permafrost that has glued the mountains together since "Earth rose out of chaos" is now melting. So with each over-heated summer the Alps are changing shape. Listen next time you go climbing or walking there, and you will hear rocks falling! Often they do so with little or no warning, as my friend Hedy and I discovered in 2006 when we were on our way to the Topali hut, perched on a narrow spur of rock way above the Mattertal.

The rib of an old moraine wall led above pastures to a wilderness of stone in the upper reaches of the Jungtal. Virtually bereft of vegetation the landscape was stark, almost intimidating. All colors were sombre—rust, dirty gray, a rather tired olive green where patches of lichen stained the rocks. Where snow patches remained from last winter they were strewn with avalanche rubble. Under heavy skies it would have been a grim place, but today the sun shone between innocent clouds and Hedy and I had no trouble retaining our optimism. When plotting our route last night Marcel, although unable to join us, had promised an interesting day. And so it would be.

We came to a small plain of silt and gravel washed by a glacial torrent. There was no bridge, so we removed boots and socks and waded through; once our feet were dry again, we continued to a small milky pool below the Junggletscher. Now we began to pick a way across an unstable slope of scree. It was purgatory, for as we slipped and stumbled so we expended far more energy than the route warranted, and it didn't take much to convince us that we'd be better off on the glacier.

We made good progress then, without crevasses to concern us, and as the glacier had no great length we soon reached the head of the icefield, where a metal ladder had been bolted to the near-vertical rock face. Hedy went up first while I followed close behind, and as we neared the top the crags to our right were suddenly bombarded by rocks of all sizes as a large section of ridge collapsed high above us. One moment the only sound to be heard was the light tap of a boot on an iron rung; the next all hell had broken loose without warning.

Instinctively we ducked our heads and hunched rucksacks for protection as the air was filled with dust and flying debris. Man-sized rocks bounded down the face, breaking more great chunks from the wall and sending stone missiles in all directions. Clinging to the ladder, there was no escape.

After a brief pause a second heavy fall followed the first. The landscape was changing before our eyes, and the sound and smell of destruction was awesome. I swear the whole rock face shook. And the ladder—and Hedy and me—with it.

When all had settled I peered down at the glacier to find our bootprints had been obliterated. Had we been a little slower, we might have been obliterated too. Hedy gave a wry smile. Her face was gleaming; dust lacquered her hair. My hands were sweaty on the ladder's uprights, and my pulse was racing. Yet by some miracle neither of us had been hurt.

Three hours later we were downing our first beers at the Topali hut—with the Mischabel peaks standing proud across the valley, Monte Rosa upvalley, Brunegghorn and Weisshorn nearby, and toy-sized houses in the Mattertal 4,500 feet below.

But the sound of falling rocks still rang in my ears; the taste of fear remained on my tongue.

Straddling a narrow rib of rock, the hut overhung the valley. Its position seemed precarious, and apart from Hedy and me few were staying there. One was a cartographer working for the Swiss national survey. Earlier that day he'd been scrambling alone on one of the Barrhorn's ridges, checking topographical detail that could not be picked up by either satellite or aerial photography. With map sheets and technical instruments spread across the table, he confessed that he loved the freedom his work gave him to spend weeks alone in the wild places, but admitted that the effects of climate change meant that it was almost inevitable that some of his work would be out of date by the time it saw print. Hedy explained about the rockfall on the far side of the Wasulicke. "Damn," he cursed. "I've only just checked that out."

"You're recording history," I told him.

"And if you're a guidebook writer," he said, raising an eyebrow, "so are you."

THE EMPEROR'S MOUNTAINS

Alone again in Austria researching more routes for a guidebook, I'd chosen to spend a few days among the Kaisergebirge in the Northern Limestone Alps. Various writing projects had taken me there before, and I'd once spent a week guiding from a base in Ellmau, where I'd noted several routes that warranted a return. Now, in what turned out to be some of the hottest days of 2007, I was checking those routes and getting to know the Emperor's Mountains a little better.

The highest summits and some of the most impressive walls of the Kaisergebirge blushed pink, crimson and gold as the sun went down. As one, all the climbers and walkers gathered on the terrace outside the Stripsenjochhaus fell silent. After a day of intense activity, this was a time of contemplation.

I was up and away early next morning, happy to be on my own, and eager to cross those mountains before the heat became too oppressive. Yet the initial descent to the start of my chosen route was not as cool or refreshing as I'd imagined it would be, for at the head of the Kaiserbachtal, and despite morning shade, the air was as dry as burnt toast following a week of high temperatures. I dared not predict what it would be like in the Steinerne Rinne, but I'd find out soon enough.

Not much more than 300 feet below the hut I left the main trail and aimed across the screes to the start of the Eggersteig, one of the earliest of all *klettersteig* protected routes that led to the great U-shaped cleft of Ellmauer Tor—the key to my crossing of this compact limestone range. Within moments of joining it I'd taken a slice out of my finger on a frayed section of cable, but once that had been cleaned and dressed with a strip of plaster I took off again and, turning a corner, found myself looking directly down several hundred feet onto the buildings of Griesalm. The exposure was sensational. And I loved it.

My route progressed up and down against the crags of the Fleischbank, and after about forty minutes it fed round to the base of the Steinerne Rinne itself. Aptly named, this narrow stone groove that rises like a monstrous seam between mountains was hemmed in by vertical or overhanging walls on which climbers were already at work. I could hear the rattle of their ironmongery and the echo of their voices above me, and could see tiny figures spread-eagled against the rock, ropes hanging free of the face where it overhung, or stretched across it to link the leader with his second where it was merely vertical. Now and again loose stones rained down the gray shaded walls to ricochet in all directions across the Rinne, and twice I had to cower under the shelter of a garage-sized boulder for protection.

The way was steep but extraordinarily well made. It clambered up rocks, slabs, and grit-covered ledges sandwiched between those mighty twin peaks, Fleischbank and Predigstuhl—the first to my right; the other soaring above on my left. But, trapped in a stone furnace and working steadily upward from one section of fixed cable to the next, sweat slithered down my nose and dripped onto the trail. My eyes stung, and after little more than an hour of this my throat was parched and rasping with dust. Half a liter of tepid water from my flask did little to quench my thirst.

At last I came to the massive gateway of Ellmauer Tor at the head of the Steinerne Rinne to gain a view out to the south—out beyond the modest green hills of the Kitzbüheler Alps, where distant white mountains of the Venediger group and the high peaks of the Zillertal Alps dazzled their glaciers and snowfields through a haze of shimmering heat. It was a restful view—so, having drained the last of my water, I lay upon an altar-like rock for a full hour, content in the belief that the most demanding part of my day was already over, and there I dozed in the sunshine with the faintest of breezes wafting through the pass.

But an hour was quite enough, so I took off again, this time downward over a long, hot tip of scree on the other side of the Tor in order to reach the start of the Jubilaumssteig, a longer and much more complex protected route than that of the Eggersteig. Although I knew of it, I'd never seen it before, let alone tackled it, and I soon found it to be full of surprises. The Jubilaumssteig demanded total concentration as I inched along the narrowest of ledges aided by wires or fixed cables, squeezed through a hole in the rock, and negotiated a way into and around a wonderland of pinnacles, towers, and turrets with plenty of space beneath my boots. Metal stanchions and iron ladders gave encouragement and led the way through a maze of bleached limestone, in which cracks and crevices hosted microscopic flower gardens. There was something unforeseen at every turn. These were not lifeless rocks, but vertical habitats upon which a whole world existed—a world unnoticed until you paused to examine it.

The way descended into a hollow, then climbed out again to emerge onto a terrace of dry grass and a blaze of crimson alpenrose, and there I spied, just a short stroll away, the Grutten hut—an old favorite, built snug against the foot of Ellmauer Halt.

In a second I forgot aching knees and torn fingers, for I could almost taste the beads of condensation running down the side of an ice-cold glass, and felt a sudden surge of energy.

Moments like these make all the effort and sweat worthwhile.

THE GIANT GREEN TORTOISE

After staggering in the heat of Austria, two weeks towards the end of summer 2007 were spent in France on the Tour of the Oisans with Jonathan Williams, my publisher. In another six weeks we'd be together in the Himalaya, but now we were making a circuit of one of the most rugged Alpine districts and enjoying once more a run of fine weather that was destined not to last.

When we turned in a full moon lit the wild amphitheater of peaks that curved around Refuge des Bans. The valley falling below the hut was revealed as a monochrome landscape with a sharp divide between light and dark, but overhead stray clouds became white vessels sailing the night sky. It would have been a good night for a bivouac, or so I thought. But two hours later I was glad of a dry bed when a storm shook the building. Thunder sounded as though the mountains were collapsing around us, and between explosions the rain was deafening on the dormitory's roof.

By morning the storm was no more than a memory. We were first up and away, leaving the hut with just enough light to dispense with headtorches. Last night the guardian had given a forecast of sunshine and cloud before midday, but the possibility of a storm in the afternoon. With more than 3,600 feet of height to gain and two passes to cross, the message was clear—don't hang around.

We didn't.

It took a little under an hour to descend to the stony plain of Entre-les-Aygues, where we stopped to readjust our loads before crossing a long wooden footbridge and weaving across the gravel flats between larch and birch trees with the first hint of autumn in their leaves. The way then rose into the Vallon de la Selle, where we had the world to ourselves, and even the old stone *cabane pastorale* of Jas Lacroix looked as though no shepherd had used it for weeks. There we stopped and ate a banana each, drank from the pipe at a water trough nearby, checked the map, estimated how long it would take to reach the first col, and reckoned we were making decent time. Another two and a half hours, give or take, and we should be on the pass, we reckoned. Without stops, that is. Then it's half hour, max, from the Col de l'Aup Martin to Pas de la Cavale, and one and a half or two hours down to the Chaumette refuge—five hours in all. Then it can storm all it likes.

We studied the sky. There was a lot of cloud, with a weak sun trying to break through, but it looked a bit suspect at the head of the valley, and the darkening gray put a rein on too much optimism. The wind had picked up too, with a few emphatic gusts that made me shiver. We continued upvalley, with our stride now a little longer and more purposeful, both with the same niggling thoughts but keeping concerns to ourselves. If only we could make it over the mountains before the weather turned.

I remembered my previous crossings, both several years ago when alone and carrying a lot more on my back than today. I recalled a succession of streams draining late-lying snow and the way the valley rose from one level to the next like a series of steps, presumably formed by glacial action. I remembered, too, the long, steep regions of black grit and scree just short of the first pass, where I'd had to dig the sides of my boots into the slope in order to cross, and where a slip would have had serious consequences.

But that was then. This is now. Today would be a piece of cake—if the weather stayed fine.

It didn't. Before we'd gone far the first spots of rain fell, so we pulled on rain gear and hurried up the trail. For a few minutes it was little more than drizzle, but neither of us was fooled by this, and as we crossed the Chanteloube tributary that drizzle turned into a full-blown downpour. We didn't break stride, but continued upvalley, rising along a stony trail that fed into a higher level of grassland. The wind came in sudden bursts, hammering the rain into our faces, its force such that no matter how good our rain gear, we were soaked within moments. I could see practically nothing through my glasses and was shivering despite the effort involved in battling the wind.

The way dropped into a hollow, then rose again, and as I emerged from it the wind struck so hard it spun me round and almost lifted me off my feet. "Bugger this," I shouted. "Let's get down to some shelter."

We ducked back into the hollow, where Jonathan pulled a nylon bivvy sheet from the top pocket of his sack. Opening it out between us and fighting the wind, we crouched on our rucksacks, pulled the sheet over us, and tucked it beneath our boots. Protected now from both the wind and the rain, within moments we felt a lot warmer.

Comparatively snug though we were, conversation was conducted at full voice, thanks to the hammering of rain on nylon, and when the wind snuck round the edge of the hollow and hit us from the side, it did so with a sudden roar that sounded like thunder. Had anyone been crazy enough to be out in this, we'd have appeared to them like a giant green tortoise whose shell rippled in the wind. Inside that shell, two adult males crouched side by side planning future book projects.

I laughed then at the bizarre nature of our situation. "Do you know of any other writer who's discussed work with their publisher when kneeling in a wet nylon shelter at over six thousand five hundred feet in the Alps?"

"Can't think of anyone off hand," said Jonathan. "I'll bet Hemingway never did."

COLLECTING SUMMITS

Perfectly set below the Matterhorn, and with its reputation for chic, Zermatt is not one of Switzerland's cheapest resorts, although notoriously impecunious British climbers have usually managed to find somewhere in town as a base they could just about afford, as have I. So it came as a great surprise when in 1997 I had a writing commission from a company that arranged all-expenses paid accommodation for me in one of Zermatt's classiest hotels. It was there that I met a well-heeled couple ticking off some of the highest of the nearby summits.

Immaculately groomed, the handsome couple with perfect complexions and outfits to match were not short of money. I suspect he might have been a banker, or an industrialist, at home anywhere in Europe; in his early fifties, top of his profession, confident and competent. She? Well, at first I thought she could be a model, or an actress, for she moved with that red-carpet assurance, aware that heads would turn. Her age was impossible to tell—anywhere from nineteen to thirty-five, she glowed with good health. The world was hers for the asking. Zermatt, of course, was just right for them both, and I imagined they would spend their days swanning from one boutique to another, diverting now and then to a chic bar or restaurant whose waiters would fall over themselves to be of service in expectation of a handsome tip. The Matterhorn was as elegant as they; it was the perfect backdrop to a perfect couple.

I'd see them most mornings as I was leaving the breakfast room. Always the first, and usually the only one there at that time of the morning, I'd be anxious to get away and out of town, checking routes for a book on behalf of the holiday company who'd arranged for me to stay there. Being more used to mountain huts or bivvies on a hillside, I found the line-up of stars on the hotel's letterhead somewhat daunting. By contrast the beautiful couple, of course, were very much at home.

Back in my room after spending a full day on the hill, I'd just have time for a shower, followed by half an hour with my toes up on the bed, then down for dinner, after which I'd be straight back to my room to write up my notes. It was usually past midnight before I'd finished these, then I'd plan my route for the next day and hit the sack exhausted.

The beautiful couple would pass my table on their way to dinner. At first they'd simply nod a recognition, but after two or three days they'd pause for a moment to speak. German, they were, but they conversed with me in English with barely a trace of an accent. They'd wish me a pleasant evening and continue to their table, where the maître d' would hold the chair for her and she'd smile her thanks. Then it would only be a matter of moments before he'd light a candle and see that they were both comfortable before offering them the menu.

On the fourth morning I'd barely left my table in the breakfast room when they waltzed in. "Good morning," he said with the brightest of voices. "Early again, I see. And where might you be off to today?"

I gave him a brief resumé of my plan; the two beamed at one another, then at me. "You must be very fit," she said, and I swallowed hard. She really was an extraordinarily beautiful woman with a voice as soft as velvet. I didn't want to embarrass them by asking which boutique they'd be exploring, so made my departure with the usual pleasantries.

That evening I was just studying the menu when they appeared beside my table. "How was your day?" he asked. "Did you achieve all you set out to do?"

"I did, thanks. Yes, another good day. And you? I hope you enjoyed your day too?"

"Thank you for asking. We did. I think I can speak for you too, Anja, yes?"

Anja, she of the beautiful face and the voice that could unnerve me, simply nodded in agreement. I'm glad she did, or my throat would have gone dry.

"We did the Alphubel," he said. "It made a very pleasant day out."

"The Alphubel!" I was impressed, then, and during the fish course tried to work out how they could have left Zermatt, say, half an hour after I'd set out this morning, climb a 13,000 foot peak, and manage to get back to the hotel in time for dinner. I know there are some pretty straightforward routes on the mountain, but even so, they'd have to be supremely fit to achieve such an ascent in so short a space of time. And they didn't look in the least as though they'd had a hard day.

Halfway through the meal I caught his glance across the room and raised my wine glass to him. He smiled and nodded his head.

The following morning we met at the breakfast-room door. I was leaving as they were just arriving, hand in hand like teenagers—or a couple on their honeymoon. "Another big day?" he asked. "Not to your standard," I replied. "What do you have planned?"

"We think either Rimpfischhorn or Breithorn," he said. "We cannot make up our minds."

I thought, "You're all bullshit," but grinned and wished them a good day—wherever they went.

Rimpfischhorn, at this time of morning, when they haven't even had breakfast! The Breithorn perhaps—but only if they take the cable car. Last night I was impressed, this morning skeptical. It just didn't add up. Or was I envious?

Again they were on time for dinner. Once again they did not appear to be unduly tired. If anything, they looked even healthier, more fresh, with added glow to their cheeks. I was ordering my meal when they came in, so they didn't stop to speak, but later I caught his eye across the room, and when I raised a questioning eyebrow he mouthed "Rimpfischhorn." Fighting skepticism I mouthed my congratulations.

The days went by and the list of 13,000 foot summits continued—Castor on Thursday, Allalinhorn on Friday. The weather was poor on Saturday and Sunday, but on Monday they claimed the Breithorn, and Pollux on Tuesday. On Wednesday they took the day off, and I was leaving for home on the Thursday. It was on that last morning that I was a few minutes late into the breakfast room. The couple were already there. With them was their guide, a mountain-tanned professional whose rope and rucksack stood beneath one of the windows. He was just finishing a cup of coffee, and as he put his cup down I overheard him tell his clients that the helicopter was standing by and could take off as soon as they were ready.

As they passed my table they stopped to say goodbye. "It was nice to meet you," he said, and they both shook my hand. Hers was tiny in mine, and I glanced down to see the diamonds on her ring flashing in the morning light.

"Where to today?" I asked.

"The big one," he said. "Mont Rosa—the noble Dufourspitze."

And I wondered how close to the summit their helicopter would deliver them.

ON THE HILL WITH HÖRST

A chance encounter in 2005 led to a commission to write some promotional material for the Carinthia Tourist Board, research for which would take place in the Karawanken mountains. Min was able to join me there, and we were allocated the services of local guide, Hörst Kaschnig, who showed us around and shared a few summits with us. When my work in Austria was finished Hörst suggested we spend a day across the border in Slovenia, where he had something to show us.

Towards the eastern end of the Alpine chain, the Karawanken carries the border between Austria and Slovenia. But a little south of those mountains, to which they are connected by limestone ribs, lies Slovenia's compact Kamnik-Savinja group, which has been likened to the nearby, better known Julian Alps but on a smaller scale. Viewed from the north, the scale is anything but small, for when you approach through the Ravenska Kocna valley you're confronted by a seemingly massive wall of rock reminiscent of the Civetta in the Dolomites, with Grintovec, its highest summit, looking magnificent at its western end.

Based in the little town of Bad Eisenkappel on the Austrian side of the mountains, Hörst was eager to introduce us to his local playground across the border. He'd already pointed out a few summits from the peak we'd climbed yesterday in the Karawanken, but nothing could prepare us for the view that burst upon us shortly after crossing the road pass of the Seebergsattel into Slovenia.

There we looked down upon a tiny hamlet, beyond which lay a green lake and a valley of idyllic meadows rimmed by forest and blocked in the south by what could only be described as an impenetrable barrier of rock. My heart took a leap. This was a view to savor.

Hörst parked the car at the end of a track in a glade of beech and fir trees, and directed our way onto the farthest left of three paths that he assured us would lead to the Kranska Koca hut. Out of the woods, unruly clumps of dwarf pine threatened to overwhelm the trail along the edge of a dried stream bed, but above them we picked a way among alpenroses in full bloom, the big walls erupting overhead in a dazzle of white and pink stone. Short sections of fixed cable, iron rungs or rustic wooden ladders gave assistance where the route mounted rocks, then the trail squeezed through a belt of vegetation before teetering along a narrow ledge.

The hut was reached in less than two hours from the woodland glade—a large, flat-roofed, three-story building looking north along the valley through which we'd approached. There we paused just long enough to catch our breath before Hörst was scampering up a stony trail that led east, up to a rib dividing two *kessels*, and continued above this onto Austria's southernmost point, the 6673 foot Seeländer Sattel. "Down there," said Hörst pointing to the north, "the Kotschnatal gives a good long walk to Eisenkappel. But I want to show you something else." And with that he took off again, almost jogging across a narrow scree path to gain a crest that marked the Austro-Slovenian border.

The Sanntaler Sattel was another great vantage point. Below to the left lay the wooded Kotschnatal; to the right the rugged Logarska Dolina valley was clamped between precipitous rock walls. Cloud shadows drifted across those walls and seduced with patches of sun-warmed limestone. "Come another time with more days to spare and we will explore down there," he urged. "The climbing is magnificent; the walking is lonely. The scenery," he added for effect, "is oh—so *wunderschön*! You would love it."

I believed him.

We retraced our path to the Seeländer Sattel, from where Grintovec dominated the view, then chased down the slope to the Kranska Koca hut for a cool drink to settle the dust. "Now to the next hut," he gestured across the face of the mountain to the west. But we'd not gone far before it became clear that the trail he claimed linked the two huts had been destroyed by rockfall. "No matter, I have another route in mind."

Down steeply we slithered between alpenrose and dwarf pine, below which the mountainside became broken by white limestone crags. Turning a spur the world fell at our feet. There was no more path, just a gully plunging into an abyss whose base we could not see. It looked as though we'd reached an impasse and would have to backtrack. Not so. One wall, I noticed, had a cable strung across it.

Hörst looked round and smiled. "You will like this," he promised, giving no opportunity for objection as he rummaged in his rucksack. Min said nothing. Despite thirty years of mountain holidays, she'd not been on a proper via ferrata before, but after shooting me a glance which said "Did you know about this?" she accepted the harness from Hörst and was soon taking instruction on the correct procedure for tackling the challenges that lay ahead.

For the next forty minutes our route traversed, climbed, and descended a series of turrets and chimneys aided by well-placed rungs, cables, and ladders. Concentration was essential, and at times 300 feet of exposure gave an adrenaline boost. But the thrill of moving safely in such a dramatic region of sun-blessed mountains was so intense that nothing could detract from it. For me, at any rate. I was not so sure about my wife.

Min remained speechless throughout, engrossed as she was with every move, her eyes scanning the rock for minor lips, grooves or projections before gingerly placing a hand or foot with Hörst's approval. He led the way and guided with care, talking her through the next few moves, his pronunciation of English words being clipped and precise despite lack of practice. He and I were not roped, but she was secured with ropes and karabiners and given confidence by our Austrian friend's smooth talking and obvious care. She'd never warmed to rock climbing, and finding herself inching across unfamiliar terrain should have had her knees trembling, but from my occasional vantage point she appeared to be in control, ignoring the verticalities by averting her eyes from the long drops—the immediate wall and its intricacies being the limit of her world. And it was only when we finally stepped onto terra firma and she slipped out of her climbing harness that she looked up at the rock face and, with eyes beaming, exclaimed: "That was great! Are there any more like that?"

MOMENTS OF BEING

Some days stand out in memory not for any specific experience but because every moment was fulfilling. Such a day came unbidden in 2004 when, after researching a series of multi-day routes with friends who had run out of time and had now returned home, I was left with a few days to enjoy on my own and a gap to fill in my knowledge of one particular section of the Swiss Alps.

The massive walls of the Daubenhorn disappeared into the clouds to cast a sombre shadow over Leukerbad. As I stepped from the bus I could tell at a glance that this old spa was not my kind of town, but I had no intention of staying long anyway, and looked for a way out. A tall, long-haired local with a ragged beard directed me past the pink marble buildings of the thermal baths, through a tunnel, and briefly along a road that gave views above the rooftops to the Gemmipass, where a roll of the clouds threatened to avalanche into the valley. A steady drizzle fell and the light was poor, but having completed three multi-day tours in the past few weeks I relished the prospect of being alone at last, with a 3,000 foot ascent to the Rinder hut to fill the afternoon.

The fact that the hut was like a concrete bunker set in the bowels of an ugly cable-car station did nothing to dampen my spirits when I arrived there. I had it to myself, and because the weather was unsettled no-one came up on the cable car either, and the couple who ran the glass-domed conservatory-like restaurant and acted as hut guardians treated me like a long-lost friend and placed a huge meal before me that evening as the clouds began to break up. An hour or so later stars lit the heavens. Tomorrow would be good, I could feel it in my bones.

It was. It dawned with a flood of light that picked out the entire chain of the Pennine Alps on the far side of the unseen Rhône valley—a sparkling parade of mountains that reached from the Mischabel group in the east to the Mont Blanc massif in the west. With heart in mouth I ran outside, eyes popping with wonder as I recognized the Weisshorn and its consort the Bishorn, the Zinalrothorn, Dent Blanche, Mont Collon, Pigne d'Arolla, the Aiguilles Rouges d'Arolla, the Combin massif and Mont Blanc itself, pure and gleaming. Summit after summit, ridge upon ridge, glacier and snowfield—each had its place in this roll call of natural wonders.

No matter how many times I'd seen those peaks, had photographed them, crossed their ridges and slept on their slopes, no amount of familiarity could lessen the impact of their beauty. Those who grow weary of the Alps have no soul. For me, each time they burst into view is cause for celebration. This morning I celebrated.

Breakfast was filling and the guardian wanted to talk, but I needed to be outside—out there with boots on feet and rucksack on back; out there sucking the cool morning air into my lungs; out there with nothing man-made between me and a ragged horizon. Out there was where I belonged.

Half an hour later a broad grass saddle removed the Rinder hut from any backward view, but ahead more mountains hitched themselves onto the eastern end of the Pennine chain, while outlying spurs of the Bernese Alps fell towards the Rhône. The map had provided a hint of what might be seen, but reality far outweighed expectation, so that every turn revealed a scene demanding reverence. I would not be found wanting on that score.

A hanging valley drew me along its pastures. At its head the Restipass seemed much closer than I'd anticipated, and for a moment I regretted its nearness, for I would have preferred a slower, more demanding approach that would delay my entrance to the Lötschental. I'd entered that glorious valley by several different ways in the past, each one demanding effort for the rewards on offer. The Lötschental deserved to be won, but the Restipass looked too easy for that. So when I reached the little Weisse See, backed by crags of the Torrenthorn, I gave in, sat among the flowers that crept towards the water, and enjoyed just *being*.

It was that sort of day.

Eventually I set off again, but my energy flagged halfway to the pass, and I almost welcomed the necessity to go slowly, to stop for frequent rests, delaying arrival at the saddle that would act as a gateway to my valley of dreams. This was a day to savor, so, pausing on the ascent, I studied the rocks, the flowers, the backward views—especially the views. I owned each one. They were mine alone, those views. These "overcrowded Alps" were secret Alps, for no-one intruded on this summer's day of exquisite beauty. The Playground of Europe had become my private domain.

The angle of the slope eased, and I could put off the inevitable no longer. Treading the last melting patches of snow on this southern flank, I stepped forward onto the Restipass. A wind picked up and rattled the rocks as the world fell at my feet where, almost 4,000 feet below, the Lötschental was revealed in all its simple grandeur. My eyes grew moist. With the wind, of course.

As impressive on this day as any Himalayan giant, off to my right the Bietschhorn acted as a gatepost beyond which a stupendous line of peaks led the eye to the icy Lötschenlücke at the head of the valley. After yesterday's rain, the light was such that distances were hard to define. Every feature in that view was sharp and clear; there were no blurred edges. The Langgletscher poked its tongue towards a wonderland of meadow and larchwood; down there a string of black villages lined the river which, from here, appeared no more than a strip of cotton. Cloud shadows scattered across the hillsides, and a flurry of birds rushed over my head with a suddenness that surprised me, their wing feathers adding to the beat of the wind.

Crouching beside the cairn that marked the pass I knew what it was to be happy. For most of us, I guess, happiness is something to strive for or to look back upon with nostalgia; the experience itself often passes without recognition. But on the Restipass I understood what a blessing life could be, and was, as I absorbed each moment and became truly aware—aware of the sudden change from wind to breeze (a kindness I could appreciate now that I'd ceased sweating); aware of the softening pulse of moving air and the smells it brought with it; aware of the drip, drip of melting snow where the sun was warming rocks behind me; aware of the far-off ring of a sheep's bell and the rasping call of a marmot.

The drama of visual beauty was obvious, for in each direction landscapes of perfection were laid bare. But there was more to this scene than that which the eye took in. Everything had its place—sound, scent, and the *taste* of the summer Alps whose flavors were captured with each intake of breath.

Life was good. Very good. I could have stayed there for ever.

HIMALAYA

Where Dreams Come True

A ll who are drawn to mountains will dream of the Himalaya, and in that I am no exception. In 1986 I took a leap of faith and began a career as a freelance writer, with self-financed research trips leading to a number of books and magazine features. Each trip was fulfilling, although not all the subsequent books covered the cost of basic research, and my long-suffering family and I lurched from one financial crisis to another. The Himalayan dream seemed destined to remain just that. A dream. Then out of the blue I was invited to trek to the south side of Kangchenjunga. The Nepalese government had just lifted access restrictions to the northeast corner of their country, and I would accompany one of the first groups ever to trek there. That was another life-changing experience.

The "once-in-a-lifetime" journey proved to be just the first of many, and nearly a quarter of a century later the exotic nature of the high Himalaya has become almost familiar. But it has not lost the power to either excite or inspire. For it is not just the mountains but the people who live among them that reward every visit and ensure a return. Again and again.

Since that first trek to Kangchenjunga subsequent visits to the world's greatest mountain range have taken me from Ladakh in the west to Bhutan in the east and many places between. Kanch has lured me back several times, not only to the north and south base camp areas in Nepal but to the Sikkimese flank too. Trekking to Everest, Annapurna, Manaslu and Langtang on writing projects, and journeys to a number of remote and little-visited regions, has only served to strengthen my love of the Himalaya and deepen my respect for its people.

Top left: The Berber goatherd who daily visited our Atlas base camp in 1965.
Top right: Young, fit and fearless, Michael Adams balances on a pinnacled ridge at almost 13,000 ft in the Atlas Mountains. *Bottom:* Berber houses cling to the hillsides like swallows' nests.

Top: Mules make backpacking unnecessary in Morocco's Atlas Mountains.
Bottom: Left foot in France, right foot in Spain—Keith Sweeting scrambles along
a ridge leading to Pic de la Mine.

Above: Enjoying solitude and pristine early-season conditions on the 10,000 ft Pico de la Maladeta.

Left: Windswept in the Pyrenees—Alan Payne and I first shared a rope in the Atlas Mountains in 1965 and subsequently made numerous expeditions to the Alps, Pyrenees and Himalaya over the next 40 years. *(Photo: Peter Smith)*

Top: The Arrémoulit refuge nestles in a Pyrenean landscape of granite and water. *Bottom:* Hugh Walton emerging from a hidden crevasse on the Vignemale's glacier. Opposite: Dawn light on the north face of the Vignemale, one of the most imposing of Pyrenean walls (Chapter 16)

Left: With the ultimate Pyrénéistes, Pierre (left) and Jean Ravier at Tuzaguet in 2006. *(Photo: Michèle Ravier)*

Below: Piz Bernina and Piz Roseg in summer—very different from a mid-winter moonlight view seen from a camp on Piz Corvatsch.

Opposite top: Glemmtal guide Fredi Bachmann, with the Hohe Tauern as a backdrop.

Opposite bottom: The ladder route to the Pas de Chèvres above the Cheilon glacier.

Top: The approach to the Mountet hut used to cross the Zinal glacier below the Ober Gabelhorn. *Bottom:* At the head of the Gasterntal, Roland Hiss studies the ice cliffs of the Kanderfirn. *Opposite top:* Shortly after dawn, the massive southwest or Yalung face of Kangchenjunga is revealed in all its glory. *Opposite bottom:* Local guide Hörst Kaschnig shows the way on a via ferrata in the Kamnik-Savinja mountains of Slovenia.

Above: Alan Payne in the Gokyo valley —our early treks in the Himalaya, using simple teahouses for accommodation, led through some memorable landscapes.

Above: Group treks rely for their success on the strength and goodwill of porters who carry the loads; they are the unsung heroes of the Himalaya.

Left: In the Langtang village of Syabru an old man watches the world go by.

Above: The four Dolpo women whose voices echoed a "song of the hidden land."
Below: A typical Sherpa house in Phortse at the mouth of the Gokyo valley.

Ploughing with buffalo—an iconic post-harvest scene in the Himalayan foothills.

On the edge of Khumjung, a solitary chorten, prayer flags and mani stones direct attention towards Ama Dablam.

Left: The silent Bhutanese woman who became my shadow on the way to Cheri Gompa.

Below Cheri Gompa stands high above the Thimpu Chhu in the Bhutanese foothills.

Top: This makeshift bridge took us across a tributary of the Buri Gandaki on my most recent trek around Manaslu. *Bottom:* My long-time friend, Kirken Sherpa (second from left), poses with our group of friends after crossing the Larkya La on the Manaslu Circuit

Above: Figures in silhouette prepare to bivouac by
a cold lake on Corsica's
Monte Rotondo.

Left: A symbolic model
ark contains the summit
book on Turkey's Mount
Ararat—sadly, Noah's signature does not appear in it.

Below: Mehmut's yayla on
the slopes of Mount Ararat.

In benevolent mood, Huascaran looks down on the memorial garden where once stood the town of Yungay.

The team of Quechua Indians and their burros that accompanied our journey around Peru's Cordillera Blanca.

ABODE OF THE GODS

It doesn't matter how many books you've read, how many photographs you've pored over, or how many lectures you've attended, the reality of the Himalaya far outweighs any expectation. So it was for me in the post-monsoon season of 1989. Childlike with wonder, I soaked up every experience and wrung each moment dry. And when we finally reached the base of the mountain we'd come to see, it was an added privilege to share the occasion with two Sherpas, for whom Kangchenjunga was as much an abode of the gods as it was for me an iconic mountain.

It had taken almost two weeks of trekking to reach the yak pasture on which our tents were pitched, and with glaciers close by I knew it would be our coldest night yet. It was, and when my bladder began to complain shortly after midnight I silently cursed the frosty air, the altitude, and the need to drink so much during the day. But when I eventually gathered up the courage to leave my sleeping bag and went outside, I was struck by the wonder of the Himalayan night sky.

A full moon cast jewels across the frosted pasture, and between an avenue of creamy peaks the heavens were flush with stars, each one diamond sharp and close enough to touch. I was even tempted to pluck a few from the sky and take them back to my tent for use as candles.

"Bed-tea" was early in that frost bowl, and having breakfasted on porridge long before the sun was up I crunched round the valley's curve to find the great white bulk of Kangchenjunga rising like a fortress at its head. The Abode of the Gods may have found daylight, but here in the ablation valley beside the Yalung glacier night still held sway, and I was thankful to be cocooned in down. On either side black slopes rose to summits anonymous in shadow, but then the corniced ridge that links Ratong with Kabru, and Kabru with Talung on the far side of the glacier, suddenly became translucent. Beyond those mountains the sun was working its magic as it climbed out of a Sikkimese meadow. In moments Talung exploded with a halo of light, and ice crystals danced in the still morning air.

Pemba waved me onto the moraine crest. A year ago he'd spent 45 days on Kangchenjunga carrying loads for a Japanese expedition and was excited to be back. He turned to Dendi and pointed out individual features on the mountain that so dominated the scene, describing the sites of Camps One, Two, and Three, and much more besides. But his words were lost on me; I was in a dream.

Jannu and Khambachen caught the sun, and having warmed their summits its light then slowly drained towards the valley. A small herd of *bharal* (the "blue sheep" that are neither blue nor sheep) skittered across a gully above us, sending down a rush of stones. The morning came alive with a dazzle of sun on snow, and the gates of heaven were opened.

I was breathless, as much with the vision before me as with the altitude, and was glad of a halt when we came to a significant *chorten* like a great milestone erected on the moraine crest above the rubble-strewn glacier. Kangchenjunga was its backdrop.

Reaching from one side of the valley to the other, the massive southwest face was displayed to perfection.

My Sherpa companions fell silent before this pile of rocks, from the top of which splayed bamboo wands wearing strips of printed cloth. A gust of wind snapped at the flags and disturbed the prayers, which were then released to the mountain deities resting on Kanch's five summits.

On a small slab tucked in the *chorten* Pemba and Dendi, being devout Buddhists, spread their gifts of rice, flower petals, and a few small-denomination rupee notes. Then turning to the mountain they chanted their prayers and flicked rosary beads with broken thumb nails—the deep voices resounding across the valley now an integral part of the mountain scene. All was as it should be.

I stood to one side, deeply moved, and when they'd finished Pemba turned to me. "Now you must pray," he commanded.

"Okay. What should I pray?"

"You pray like we do. That you come back again."

So I did.

And those prayers were answered, for I have been back. Many times.

TEN THOUSAND PRAYERS IN THE WIND

If mountains are the initial attraction for the majority of first-time visitors to the Himalaya, the impact of local people and their culture is the main reason for a longing to return. Trekking in the Annapurna range in 1991, Alan Payne and I were struck by the variety of different ethnic groups we met in the villages we passed through, and when we hired a local man to accompany us for a few days, he added to our understanding of the way of life of some of his neighbors.

Above Pisang, on the northern side of the Annapurnas, our trail took us from one ancient village to another. In one we were enticed up a log-hewn ladder and through a low doorway to be swallowed by the darkness of a smoke-filled room, where an old man with a woolen hat pulled over his scalp stirred a blackened pot of *tsampa*. Without a word he nodded that we should sit, then mumbled something to Mahdri, our local guide. The two men laughed, our host's voice crackling with phlegm.

A tiny slit-like window allowed light into the room and some of the smoke to leave. A faint blue beam angled from window to floor, picking out the gentle swirl of smoke and dancing dust fairies. The walls were bare, black, and shiny with the soot of who knows how many years of open fires. The only furnishings were the rugs on which we sat and a pair of long, thick cushions against the wall beneath the window.

Tibetan salt-butter tea was poured into surprisingly delicate cups and handed to us. The first sip was a shock, for it tasted nothing like Earl Gray or PG Tips. Then I remembered that if you think of it as soup rather than tea, the taste is much more palatable. Subsequent sips certainly tasted better than the *tsampa*, which not only looked like warm clay but had a similar flavor and consistency. Mahdri was offered some. He scraped a stick around the inside of the pot, drew it out, pulled the goo through his fingers, rolled it into a ball, and tossed it into his mouth.

Both Mahdri and the old man scraped at the pot again and again, rolling tsampa into balls and popping them into hungry mouths. When they'd finished, our guide was handed a jug which he held above his tilted head to pour water into his mouth. None touched his lips and not a drop was spilled, and above the crackling fire I could hear the gulping sounds as he swallowed.

As we left the village a big black Tibetan mastiff came towards us from a side-path, its lips curled, hackles raised. Instinctively I picked up a stone as my only defence. The dog bellowed; its wooly back arched, head thrust forward it fixed me with its yellow eyes, venomous teeth bared. Mahdri swore at it and hurried away without taking his eyes off the creature for a single second. My skin prickled as I imagined those teeth tearing at my flesh and the slow horror of death by rabies.

But the moment was gone, and for no apparent reason the animal backed away, barking in frustration.

Passing to the left of a *chorten* and a *mani* wall as old as history, we soon came to a water-driven prayer wheel encased in a stone shed, the prayer wheel half the height of a man and faded with age. A small stream ran down the mountainside and was directed beneath the shed, where it turned a paddle that spun the wheel. The drum of this prayer wheel was packed tight with papers inscribed with the Buddhist mantra, "Om mani padme hum." Above it there hung a small bell, and with each revolution a projecting arm would strike it, announcing to all within hearing that the air was thick with prayers.

Ten thousand "Om mani padme hums" accompanied our journey, while across the valley two Annapurnas, one Lamjung Himal, and an ice-bound Gangapurna, reached for the sky.

CULTURE SHOCK

I'm constantly amazed at the number of people whose only exercise has been to take the dog for a walk round the block, but who on a whim sign up for a multi-day trek to Everest Base Camp. In the autumn of 1999 we met an Australian woman who had not only been uninterested in walking or travel of any kind, but had never even been out of the state in which she lived. It should have come as no surprise, then, that she was totally unprepared for what she discovered on arrival in Nepal.

Brought up in Perth, Alice Carera had never been out of Western Australia, but after watching a film about Mount Everest on television she was fired with a girlish, unbridled enthusiasm and a yearning for adventure. Within a few days she'd encouraged a friend to join her, found a Kathmandu agent on the internet, and booked a four-week trek to Everest Base Camp with a guide and two porters to accompany them.

She had no idea what she'd let herself in for.

We met her in a lodge in Shivalaya at the end of our first day on the trek from Jiri. Rocking gently back and forth, she sat in a corner hugging herself—not through cold, but in despair. Her face wore a haunted, lost expression; her eyes were red-rimmed and baggy; her hair needed attention; and it looked as though she'd lost the will to live. In vain her friend was trying to entice her to eat something. While ignoring the drama going on behind them, their guide and porters were in lively conversation with our man, Krishna.

"Look Alice, you can't go on like this. You gotta eat something."

Alice was tall and well built, in her late forties, I'd guess, and not addicted to a carrot and lettuce diet, by the look of it. Glum-faced she said nothing but shook her head from side to side, reminding me of a petulant teenager. Then slowly she stood up, walked across the room, and the next moment her heavy feet could be heard on the wooden stairs.

"Jeez, I give up." Her friend came over to Min and me. "Where you guys from?" she asked. "England," we said.

"You been here before? To Nepal?"

"A few times."

"Hev you ever come across anyone like Alice?" she gestured towards the stairs.

"How d'you mean?"

"Culture shock, I guess you'd call it. We arrived in Kathmandu five, no, six days ago. In the taxi from the airport to our hotel she freaked out. She just couldn't take it—the crowds, the noise, the smell, the whole bloody anarchy of the place. Me? I thought it bizarre, but I've been around a bit and seen a few things. Not Alice. She was spooked. I mean, really spooked, shaking so much that when we got to the hotel she refused to go out again. I had to do everything. Everything! I had to deal with the agent, get the money, organize permits, the whole bloody lot. She just sat in our room staring at the floor. Wouldn't eat anything 'cept biscuits; wouldn't drink anything 'cept Coke."

"Coupla days ago," she continued, "I managed to prise her outa the hotel and into a minibus taxi; Alice n'me and the boys there. In the scrum to get out of town she sank into the back seat with a scarf over her face. Stayed like that 'til we were out in the country and there were no more beggars banging on the windows, no more cows in the streets chewing on black plastic bags, no more hunks of raw meat covered in flies on street corners, and the incessant honking of horns had slackened off a bit. But you know what the road's like. Like it's been shelled by artillery, with bloody great potholes everywhere, so the driver's either slamming into them and shakin' the shit out of you, or swerving about like he's on some crazy slalom. Then there's the trucks driven by madmen who wanna overtake on a blind bend. And the buses—oh, Jeez, you draw alongside one and there's always someone puking down the sidev'it. I mean, that ain't normal in Perth."

Min and I grinned at one another. The Aussie was describing it perfectly. To get to Jiri we had not bothered with a taxi this time, but had ridden for 12 hours on a crowded public bus shared with livestock as well as half the population of Kathmandu. It had been one of life's experiences. It always was. Colorful, you had to admit.

"Name's Christine," and she offered a hand. "Sorry to go on about it, but Alice has just about lost it n'I dunno what to do. If she won't eat we ain't gonna get far. And there's no way she'll get back in a taxi or on a bus to return along that road. Jeez, what a mess! She's a mother of four teenage kids; a geography teacher and an intelligent woman. Or so I thought. It was she who talked me into coming here, and now it looks like we ain't gonna get anywhere. And you know what? I really wanna see Everest now. It was Alice who fired me with enthusiasm, but soon as we get off the plane it's like the life's gone out of her. What a mess. What a right bloody mess!"

I thought about her dilemma for a minute or two, then had an idea. We still had a couple of apples we'd brought from home. "What room is she in?" I asked.

"Just above here. Top of the stairs, first on the right. Why?"

"This might help." I pulled one of the apples from my rucksack, handed it to Min, and suggested she go upstairs and see if Alice would take it. "It's worth a try."

It did. It worked like a charm. Min sat on the bed with her, offered the apple—a crisp Cox's orange pippin. She told Alice where it came from, said she was welcome to have it. Alice wiped her face with the back of her hand, took the apple with a half-smile, and bit into it. Apparently juice ran down her chin. "Come and join us when you've finished," said Min. "It'll be good to talk."

That evening we encouraged her to have a bowl of noodle soup. She managed half of it, but that was a start. Christine caught my eye and gave a wink. The following morning I told them we'd be going to Bhandar, and if they got that far we'd look out for them. They did, and after managing a few fried potatoes and an egg in the lodge there (grimacing, it must be said) Alice began to talk about happenings along the trail, the things she'd seen, the effort involved in climbing to the settlement of Deorali on the ridge overlooking Bhandar. If she found that demanding, I thought, wait until she gets to Namche—if she gets that far. But she was opening up, losing her lost look, her resignation. There was hope after all.

We didn't walk with them during the day, but met them each evening and were pleased to see that as time went on Alice was becoming much more attuned to the trek, to life on the trail, and happy to notice what was going on in villages without finding them too scary, too uncomfortably alien. She was eating a little more each day, and by the time we'd reached Junbesi the two Aussies were almost like seasoned trekkers. "How did you cope with the Lamjura La?" I asked. "Piece of cake," said Alice.

I told them we'd be spending two nights here, for I wanted to visit the Thubten Chholing Gompa that stood upvalley, and suggested that if they were in no hurry to move on, they should join us. They did. We walked there on a day of sparkling clarity, watching butterflies the size of wrens drifting about the valley, noting forests of prayer flags stretching up the hillsides, and talking with monks and novice monks at the monastery. But on the way back to our lodge I foolishly asked Alice about her family. With that she burst into tears. A longing to see her husband and boys again suddenly overwhelmed her. Gone were the joys of discovery she'd just begun to experience. Gone was the resurrected dream of seeing the highest mountain on earth. Instead, she could think only of the familiar back home. And she missed it all.

Not for the first time in my life I should have used my brain and kept my big mouth shut.

Next morning, when Min and I were planning to move on, Christine came down to breakfast without Alice. "She won't get out of bed. She's lying in her sleeping bag with her head covered by a sweater. Sobbing. Just sobbing. Won't even talk to me. I can't get any sense out of her, and I've had it up to here. It's no good, she just wants to be home."

"Well, you've got an opportunity to arrange that," I told her. "Half a day's walk from here there's an airstrip at Phaplu, with flights to Kathmandu. You might be able to get her on one."

"Fat chance," she said. "I can't even get her out of bed."

So I went upstairs, walked into her room, pulled the sweater from Alice's face, and ordered her to get up. "There's a bowl of hot porridge waiting downstairs, and if you get your finger out, you might even get a flight back to Kathmandu in the morning. With luck you could be in Perth by the weekend."

Ten days later we bumped into Christine in Tengboche. She was on her way to Everest Base Camp with a guide and a porter, looking fit and relaxed. A big smile spread across her face and her eyes glowed. "What news of Alice?" I asked.

"Good," she said. "You were right. When we got to Phaplu I managed to phone our agent in Kathmandu. He met Alice off the plane, saw her to the hotel, and even arranged to get her a seat on a flight to Bangkok with a connection to Perth. Like you said, she was home by the weekend. Now I can enjoy the trek without culture shock getting in the way."

GURU WITH AN EMPTY DOKO

For those who wish to gain more than just photographs of their travels, trekking in the Himalaya opens up many opportunities for learning. Leaving any preconceived notions of superiority at home, keeping an open mind, and being prepared to listen are all crucial. In 1991 I found myself learning from an unexpected source.

Returning alone from the Annapurna Sanctuary I fell in step with a Gurung farmer who'd delivered a load to a Korean expedition and was now on his way home with an empty *doko*. He spoke some English and was keen to practice, so we conversed staccato fashion as we trod the damp trail together through the Modi Khola's gorge. He told me about his family and the few fields in which he grew millet, pumpkins, bananas, and oranges. He told me there was no money to be made from farming, so when the opportunity arose he would become a porter and carry loads for expeditions and sometimes, but not often ("few many" he said), for trekking parties. That way he could earn cash.

"What do you do in the winter," I asked, "when the fields are bare and there are no expeditions to carry for?"

"I sit," was his answer.

Perhaps he did not understand my question, so I tried again. "Tell me," I said, and we stopped on the path while I caught my breath, for it was not easy to string detailed sentences when every step along the way needed full concentration. "Tell me—there will be times when there are no expeditions to carry for, and no work to do in the fields. Yes?"

"Yes."

"What do you do then? How do you live your days?"

"Oh yes. I sit."

"You sit!"

"I sit. Yes, sir, I sit."

Only slowly did the truth dawn upon me. This man, whose name I did not know but who was my friend for an hour, this man felt no urge to do anything but sit—for days at a time! We in the West are unable to do this without guilt; we must always be doing something—working, reading, discussing, watching television even. But we must *do something*. The East is different. Time has other meanings, priorities or values we cannot grasp. So my friend was content just to sit. His eyes gleamed, his mouth smiled, and his high cheekbones were tight against the walnut skin.

Thousands of feet above us the fish-tail summit of Machhapuchhre disappeared into cloud, as for an hour along a damp mountain trail I slowly perceived another tempo of life. And a bare-legged farmer became my guru.

• • •

THE PUJA ROOM

In the high Himalayan valleys many villages support a Buddhist gompa of some antiquity. Prayer flags protect houses and are bleached by the winds on a remote pass; mani stones are built into walls; chortens and stupas add grace to a wild landscape. And sometimes a door is opened to welcome a stranger to a puja room to sample the spirituality within. In 1994 such a door was opened for me.

Having spent days camped among the glaciers near the head of the Langtang valley, the thicker air, lush vegetation, and agreeable warmth of Syabru gave an excuse for a rest. Preparations were being made for a Buddhist ceremony, and I'd spent most of the day by the *gompa* watching as one of the monks fashioned a figure out of clay and an old woman with a goitre padded to and fro with a kettle of *chang*, filling earthenware cups, and handing out boiled potatoes to rub in a dish of chili paste. On a terrace below the *gompa* a group of men and women threshed rice with bamboo flails, the rhythmic "thrap, thrap, thrap" of their labours drifting up the slope.

As evening slid gently into the hills, half a moon rose from a distant valley to float among long wisps of cloud. Different sounds then filtered through the village—the grumbling of a buffalo, a massed choir of insects, bamboo wind-chimes caught by a November breeze, the gentle slap as a prayer flag shook out its mantras. Down in the valley a dog barked at the moon.

The *didi* at our lodge put aside her weaving to prepare the meal, and by candlelight she served garlic soup, followed by a great dome of rice with daal and bitter spinach. We washed it down with Star beer, then sat outside gazing across the valley to snow mountains that rose above wooded hills.

Amit joined us and squatted shyly beside Alan. He'd been a

great asset to us, this diminutive Rai hillsman from eastern Nepal. He'd carried our tent, cooking equipment and food for the high camps, and taught us a lot about the customs and beliefs of his country. Quiet, strong, and dependable, he had made the transition from porter to friend in no time and had opened doors for us, both in the literal sense and metaphorically.

"You hear bell?" he suddenly asked.

We listened. And sure enough, the tinkling of a bell came wafting along the street. Not only the sound of a bell, but a deep humming. A voice at prayer.

"From the *gompa*?"

"No," said Amit. "I go see."

Two minutes later he reappeared and, without a word, signaled for us to join him. With that he turned round and headed back towards the monastery. But we didn't get that far. Using the headtorch we'd given him he took us into a house and up a flight of wooden stairs. Yellow light outlined a door on the landing. He pushed it open, and there we could see into the *puja* room, where an elderly man was seated cross-legged behind a low table on which a row of butter lamps flickered. The old man was mumbling a hypnotic chant and, without pausing for a moment, glanced up at us and nodded his head, which we took to be an invitation to join him. Amit directed us to a shelf-like seat covered with a blanket, and the three of us sat down.

A framed picture of a Buddhist saint was propped against the back wall with brightly colored strips of tapestry hanging on either side. A *thanka* was pinned to the right-hand wall, the intricacies of the mandala painting too small and distant to be seen from our seat.

On the unpolished table lay a thick block of Buddhist text from which the old man was reading aloud. In his left hand he held a small brass bell, which he rang at regular intervals. With his right hand he picked grains of corn from a tin plate, then dropped them one by one into a small brass container against which a postcard of the Dalai Lama was leaning. Now and again he'd add some liquid from an old Sprite bottle to a small dish. The heads of four marigolds drooped over the edge of a glass jar; a stick of incense smouldered.

The old man swayed gently to the rhythm of his prayers, which filled the room. Strange sounds they were. Strange to our Western ears; the words meant nothing that we could decipher. But that didn't matter. Ignorance was no barrier here. The old man was at peace with his faith, such that his door was open to non-believers. We sat with hearts and minds open, for we had come to his country not to judge but to learn; to fill our days with experience, not only among the glaciers of the high mountains, but among the gentle folk who filled the spaces with their prayers. The old man's unself-conscious reverence was another lesson.

CLEVER LITTLE SOD

Kathmandu never fails to surprise, entertain, amuse, and annoy in equal measure. It's colorful and polluted, anarchic, chaotic and overcrowded, and evidence of appalling deprivation is seen alongside the most elegant architectural features. A thousand traders offer identical goods for sale, "genuine" items made in Chinese back streets flood the markets, and every day a new scam hits the streets, as I discovered one morning in 2002 shortly before heading for the hills.

After many years of visiting the Himalaya I thought I'd grown streetwise to the ways of the East, so when the wide-eyed urchin approached me in a Kathmandu back street I was alert and wary. I'll usually give a few coins to beggars, but the place is lively with scams.

"Mornin sir, which country from?"

"England." Keep it brief, I told myself, continue walking, and whatever you do avoid eye contact.

"Good country, England," he said, with all the certainty of someone who visits twice a year. "Ask me capital city."

"I don't need to ask. I know it."

"Yes sir, but I know too. Capital city London. Houses of Parleymint, Big Ben, Queen Lizbiff. Ask nuther. Any country, I give capital city."

I moved away, ignoring him.

"Go on sir, any country, I know capital."

"Nigeria." That would stump him, I thought. But none of it, for quick as a flash he responded: "Abooojah! See, you thought I say Lagos. But I know. Me clever little sod."

"You are that," I agreed. "So how about Slovenia?"

"Easy. Loobeeyarna. Ask me difficult one."

I was being sucked in. Warning bells were ringing, but the cheeky little kid had swallowed a world atlas and was ready to spew its contents. "Maldives," I said. "Marrleee" came back with a gurgle of delight. "Croatia?" "Zaaargreb." "El Salvador?" "San Salvador." "Fiji?" "Sooova." I couldn't say if he was right, but no doubt he was. There were no flies on this little lad.

"If you're so dammed clever, why aren't you at school?"

"No money for school," he said sadly, and I thought—here we go, he's set the trap, but I'm not going to fall into it.

"Farva dead. Muvva got sick, baby sister sick. No work, no money, no food, no medsin, no school." I wouldn't look at him, but could imagine the pathetic, near-tearful expression, the hand held out for a few rupees.

Just ignore him and keep walking.

"Don't worry sir," the eight-year-old was saying through the blast of car horns and ringing of rickshaw bells, "Not wanting money."

"That makes a change," I heard a voice respond. It sounded just like my own. But I'd vowed to ignore the kid.

"Money no good to me."

"Why not?" That familiar voice again; why didn't it stay silent?

"Cos big boys beat me up and steal it."

"Really? What are you after then?"

"Just practiss English. Sool."

"Well, you're doing very well." And like an idiot I looked at him. Only for a brief second, but that was it.

"F'you really wanted to help. Only f'you wanted to," he said walking sideways knowing that this old fool was wavering. "F'you wanted to, to stop baby sister dying"—and the harps began to play—"she needs milluk. Muvva's milluk gone dry cos she's sick. No money f'me. Juss milluk. Sool."

"Where d'you imagine I'm going to find milk here?"

"Powder, sir. In tin. Shop in nekstreet." And I found myself being guided round the corner where, rather conveniently, there stood a small pharmacy. "Here sir," he said. "Speck milluk powder here."

There was. Just one tin of powdered milk on a shelf above the counter.

The shop keeper never twitched an eyelid, ignored the child beside me, took my money, and handed the tin over.

The bare-footed lad was full in his gratitude, and for a fraction of a second I imagined the eyes of his sick mother brighten with relief as her son handed over the tinful of hope so the tiny daughter could live another day or two. Here in Nepal it costs little to feel momentarily like a saint. A warm glow radiated from me as I watched him disappear among the chaos of traffic, then resumed my journey to Swayambhunath.

That warm glow lasted all of two minutes until the penny dropped. I wondered then how many times that tin of milk would be sold and bought back in just one day. Enough, of course, for it to be the only item in the shop not covered with a layer of dust.

A beggar would have been satisfied with a few rupees, but I'd just forked out a hundred times that amount.

Another mug had been sucked in. Clever little sod!

THE WONDER OF A BLUE FRONT DOOR

It doesn't take much to lift a man's day, as became evident while trekking the Annapurna Circuit in 1991. All it takes is knowledge of the color of his brother's front door in a country he's never visited. Just the color.

Once a caravanserai for traders carrying goods to and from Tibet, the village of Tukuche on the right bank of the Kali Gandaki was now a shadow of its former self, but a few of the larger buildings had found fresh use as trekkers' lodges, and one looked especially inviting.

We entered an inner courtyard bright with flowers in tubs. Nasturtiums with long trailers of orange and sun-yellow heads adorned pots spaced up an outer stairway that led to the flat roof where we settled at a table out of the wind, with a view across the rooftop to the three wavelike Nilgiri peaks.

"From England?" asked the lodge owner. Then: "Do you know Ealing?"

"Not really," I told him. "I've been there, but I wouldn't say I know it."

Undeterred our host explained, "My brother lives in Ealing." He hovered close to our table, hopeful that I might remember the place well. "Ealing," he repeated. "England, Yew Kay."

"Sorry, no."

We ordered food, delighted with the architecture of the building, the care with which it had been maintained, the charm of its flower tubs—and the view across the valley, where ice on the face of one of the Nilgiri peaks flashed the sun at us like a mirror. Moments later a lone trekker arrived and sat at the table next to ours. We exchanged trail information; he was going upvalley, we were descending.

The lodge owner reappeared and, hearing us conversing in English, he immediately turned to the newcomer. "Excuse me sir, do you know Ealing?"

The lone Englishman flashed a glance at us as if to say—what's this about? "Sure," he said, "I used to live there."

"Ooh, you live there!" The Thakali man's face brightened with anticipation.

"No, I *used* to live there, until two or three years ago. Why?"

"My brother lives in Ealing." And with that the lodge owner scurried down the stairs and returned a couple of minutes later clutching a small notebook. Thumbing through it he came upon his brother's address and handed it over. "There," he said, trembling with excitement. "Ealing!"

"Hey, I know that street. It's just round the corner from my mum's place! Let me see, number thirty-four." The Englishman paused and the lodge owner held his breath. "Thirty-four . . . Yeah, got it. It's the one with the blue front door."

"Ooh! Ooh! My brother has a blue front door!" And with that the lodge owner clapped his hands, spun around, and clapped his hands again. "A blue front door!" he repeated, hopping from one foot to the other, then scampered to the kitchen to inform his wife.

----------▲----------

THE ULTIMATE CHAPATTI

Few would visit the Himalaya for a gourmet experience, and although it's rarely necessary to go to the extremes adopted on his pre-war expeditions by Bill Tilman, with his notoriously bland diet, you grow used to living on a restricted choice of food. But on occasion a surprise ingredient adds a little spice to even the simplest chapatti, as I experienced on a cold November day in 1993.

The yakherd's face was flat and round, with high cheekbones, and dark eyes. Framed by jet-black hair pulled tightly behind her ears and held down with a cotton scarf, it had been scorched by high altitude, sun, and wind. It was difficult to tell her age, but my guess would be mid to late thirties. Her hands were larger and more masculine than the short body would suggest; they were cracked, dry, and white with flour as she kneaded the dough for my chapatti, rocking to and fro beside the yak-dung fire whose acrid smoke made my eyes sting. She sniffed and coughed and gave me a sly glance, and when our eyes met she quickly looked away, with a smile creeping from the corners of her mouth.

The door was open, despite the fact that the little stone-built hut stood at almost 14,700 feet, and through it I could see the damp mist of November creeping along the valley, hiding the mountains from view. I leaned closer to the fire, hands open to receive its warmth, but caught a face full of smoke for my pains. I turned away, choking on the ripe smell of burning dung. The *didi* chuckled and muttered something which sounded like: "English no like Sherpa air!"

On the contrary, this English was more than happy with Sherpa air, so long as it was outdoors. But out there it was getting a little thin at these altitudes, which is why today we'd had a trek of less than three hours—it was unwise to gain too much height too quickly until we'd acclimatized. And we weren't properly acclimatized just yet. Hence our early arrival at the yakherd's hut, which we'd discovered standing on a square of pasture surrounded by drystone walls. Out there, three of the shaggy beasts were snuffling and snorting as the mist clung to their coats and fixed them with drops of moisture that in another couple of hours would no doubt turn to ice.

We'd arrived in the sunshine of midday and been captivated by the setting. An amphitheater of rock peaks formed a backdrop. A narrow tributary valley cut by a stream spilled from it, and where this tributary entered the main valley a high bench of pasture had been abruptly leveled by a glacier that was now drawing back to its roots in the north. In all directions mountains of 19,000 to 20,000 feet jostled for attention. But now they were disappearing from view, swallowed by thickening mist.

The *didi* spread the chapatti dough on a flat stone and began to roll it out. She then peeled it off and slapped it from one hand to the other. At that moment one of her yaks thrust its head through the open door.

"Pssht! Tscho, tscho!" The Sherpani dropped the dough, threw an imaginary stone at the yak, then hastened to the door where she beat the animal on the head and pushed it away. "Tscho, tscho, pssht!"

As the beast backed away it left a steaming deposit on the doorstep.

Waste not, want not, the *didi* scooped up the fresh warm dung in her bare hands and slapped it on the wall to dry, then padded back to the fire, wiping her hands on her striped *chuba*, and resumed the job of kneading my chapatti dough.

It was the tastiest chapatti I'd ever eaten.

A TASTE OF BEAUTY

Most of us take the gift of sight for granted. But imagine how different our experience of the world would be without visual perception; we'd be forced to compensate for the lack of sight with our other senses. In the springtime of 2001 I organized a Himalayan trek for a friend who had become all but blind. It turned out to be one of the most fulfilling and educational of all my Himalayan travels.

As long as I'd known Ray his sight had been poor, but it had never stopped him doing the things he loved, and each summer he'd go trekking in the Alps with a couple of friends to act as his eyes. He was okay on level ground, could just about cope with uphill trails, but he found every downhill step difficult to gauge. So his friends did the seeing for him. Then his sight went completely in one eye, leaving the other so badly weakened as to be next to useless.

"My only regret," he told me one day, "is that I never got to the Himalaya."

"What's to stop you?" I asked. And with that we began to plan a multi-day journey across the mountains. Just four of us went, along with our man, Kirken, and his crew of Sherpas and porters.

Beginning at Gorkha we spent twenty-four days trekking across the Manaslu foothills, up and over the Ganesh Himal, into the Langtang valley, then over the Laurebina La and down through the terraces of Helambu to Kathmandu. Twenty-four days of Himalayan Blind Man's Bluff, with Ray "seeing" the landscape not with his eyes, but through his other senses.

Sharing the trails with him taught me that sight can make you blind.

How come?

With the gift of sight a whole landscape may be captured with a single glance. Memories are dominated by visual images; they're almost one dimensional. But without sight, it will be sounds, scents, and touch that come to the fore. My journey with Ray gave a deeper and more profound understanding of the world around us. He'd trail a hand against rocks, shrubs, and trees that lined the path. He'd pause with head tilted to one side, and I'd realize he was listening to something. So I'd listen too, and capture the sound of a bird or insect, or perhaps a distant stream or the breeze ruffling leaves; sounds I may otherwise have missed.

I was aware of his nostrils detecting the fragrance of a flower or the earthy smell of a terrace newly turned by a wooden plough dragged by buffalo. He knew before we did that we were approaching a teahouse or a village still some distance away. And having been a tree specialist all his working life, he knew which species we were passing by simply touching their trunk with his fingertips.

The Sherpas and porters loved and admired him. Maila had the job of guiding him, holding onto his arm when the trail was rough or exposed, or when we crossed snowfields or rivers on two-plank footbridges. Without any communal language the two developed an understanding. Having made several treks already with Maila, my respect for his patience grew. As for Ray, my friend was transformed into a hero.

It was springtime, and towards the end of our journey we found ourselves in a rhododendron forest. The pink-barked trees towered as high as an English oak, but unlike oak trees the rhododendrons were slim-trunked, their branches less numerous, and the flowers that blazed from them ranged from white through magnolia pink to a deep crimson. Between the trees, snow peaks of the Himalayan arctic wall were distant reminders of days now behind us. Spokes of light angled across our path, and Ray was stepping through Venetian blinds of sunshine and shadow. But it was the headlamp-sized flowers that captured our imagination, for every tree was garlanded with color — colors that Ray could not see.

Maila had a brainwave. Indicating that Ray should stand still and wait, he went from tree to tree gathering blossoms, then carried them carefully back to our friend. The nectar from each flower was poured into his cupped hands, then Maila told him to drink.

Although unable to see their colors, Ray was able to taste their beauty. And as he did, a tear slid down his cheek.

HEAD-TO-HEAD IN THE HIMALAYA

At the end of a trek in Sikkim some years ago, a Dutchman staying in the same foothill hotel was sent by his wife to ask me how trekkers cope in the mountains so far as toilets are concerned. He was embarrassed to ask the question, but curious enough to wait for the answer as I briefly described the little tent perched over a freshly dug hole. What I didn't explain is what happens when there's only one toilet tent but two people in dire need at the same time, as occurred one bitterly cold night in 2004.

It's useful, if not essential, for an author to have a good working relationship with his publisher, and it helps if both author and publisher share a common passion for the subjects they work with. In our case, mountains. Trekking together enabled Jonathan and me to build an understanding in the most unexpected ways.

Imagine Nepal. Picture the highest and most visually dramatic mountains on Earth—summits that pierce the deep Himalayan blue; mountains of exquisite grandeur; peaks strung one to another by lofty pelmets of snow and ice; glaciers tumbling in a series of motionless cascades; deep troughs filled with ice, flanked by soaring walls of moraine; and, caught in an ablation valley between moraine wall and mountain slope, a string of turquoise lakes that by day sparkle in sunshine and by night are silenced by a coating of frost-made glass.

Imagine snow—deep and crisp and even snow spread in a carpet with a sun-dazzle that pains the eyes and scorches any exposed skin unprotected by a thick coating of cream.

Imagine a pile of rocks topped by bamboo wands from which colored prayer flags dance in the breeze. As darkness falls, each flag stiffens with a rime of frost. The temperature plummets. At

15,500 feet, almost the height of Mont Blanc's summit, November chill grips the valley.

Despite the cold and the particles of frost that glistened on the inner walls of my tent, my sleeping bag made a snug nest of down. Within it I was cocooned in cozy thermal layers and did not want to leave its comfort. The last thing I wanted to do was crawl out of that bag a couple of hours after midnight and pull on down jacket, trousers over my long johns, and cold, stiff boots on my feet. I dreaded the prospect of traipsing through the frost by the light of my headtorch to crouch in that canvas sentry box of a toilet tent—known out here as the *chaarpi*.

I didn't want to. But the need was compelling.

I'll spare you the details. But the reason for my 2am hike had not been fully accomplished when the silence was broken by the sound of a tent door being unzipped. There was an urgency about that sound. It was not slow and gentle, tackled with a determination not to disturb others. No. This was the sudden noise of desperation, followed by the scampering of unlaced boots across frozen ground. With the glow of a headtorch coming my way.

I was in a quandary. For my own peace of mind I needed another minute. That was all. But the fast-approaching sound told me that someone else did not have a minute to spare. There was an urgency to it that would brook no discussion; his need was clearly greater than mine and I had better get out of the sentry box. And fast.

We met head-on as we both fumbled with the same zip. I from inside, he from outside. This was no time for pleasantries. I erupted from the *chaarpi* as he burst in. My long johns were halfway up. His were halfway down.

Moments later, as I adjusted my clothing and gazed up at the Himalayan night sky, whose stars were close enough to touch, I began to laugh as I imagined a headline in an outdoors magazine. It read: "Author and publisher in head-to-head over *chaarpi* rights in the high Himalaya."

THE KHUMBU CARPENTER

Trekking from gompa *to* gompa *in the early spring of 2008, I spent a couple of nights in a lodge run by the wife of a climbing Sherpa who spent his valley-based days working as a carpenter. His mother also lived at the lodge, and it soon became evident that she had concerns shared by the mothers of countless high-altitude climbers of all nationalities.*

Although the temperature was hovering just a degree above freezing, the Sherpa was working outdoors with shirt sleeves rolled up. He had a short length of timber laid upon the drystone wall outside his home, the timber held down by a couple of rocks while he ran a plane along its edge. He worked in an efficient manner, each stroke of the plane smooth and unhurried, and if the timber showed sign of movement, he'd steady it with his knee. Curled wood shavings fell around his Nike trainers; a few snagged on his woolen socks.

Behind him the house had been enlarged and adapted for use as a trekkers' lodge, run by his wife, while his mother, a diminutive woman in a striped *chuba*, navy down jacket, and matching woolen hat pulled tight over her jet-black hair, drifted back and forth flicking her rosary beads and mumbling quietly to herself. Or was she praying? When the stove lost some of its heat she would pad outside, collect frozen yak dung from the enclosure next door, scoop up a handful of wood shavings, and return to pour the fuel into the stove. Then, empty handed, she'd return to the curtain-covered door and spin the prayer wheel fitted beside it. When darkness fell, she'd be dwarfed by a pile of rugs and cushions in the corner, positioned next to what could be termed an altar. On it were butter lamps, a small shiny bowl of water, and a postcard of the Dalai Lama.

The old lady was not as old as she appeared, but her face, not much bigger than a child's, had been furrowed by years of anxiety. Phurba talked with her and learned that her husband—father of the carpenter—had been a high-altitude porter who earned good money carrying loads on Everest for foreign expeditions. He'd been ambitious, learned to speak several languages, and summited the mountain twice. The second time he never returned, leaving his four-year-old son fatherless.

The old lady found it difficult to come to terms with her loss, and even more difficult when her only son also became a high-altitude Sherpa—the walls of the room were decorated with framed photographs and certificates recording his achievements on an impressive list of big Khumbu summits. For years she had tried to dissuade him from going onto the mountains. Why couldn't he be content to earn a living as a carpenter? He could have a good life without the dangers faced by icefall, crevasse or avalanche. Did he really need more money?

Her arguments fell on deaf ears. Between expeditions he would work with plane, chisel, and saw, but when the climbing seasons came around, he'd fill a rucksack and walk out of the door. She never knew if he would return. Neither did the carpenter's wife. The two women tried to keep their fears to themselves. But day by day, whether her son was home or away, the old lady would tell her rosary, spin the prayer wheel, and hope the spirits would be kind.

OLD MAN VERY TIRED

It's easy to become so absorbed and excited by a dramatic landscape that you forget to pace yourself and race from viewpoint to viewpoint, impervious to altitude and the limitations of middle age, and almost imagine you're indestructible. So it was in the post-monsoon season of 1991 when, after completing the Annapurna Circuit, my trekking partner continued down to Pokhara for a spell of R&R, leaving me to chase around the lower hills and up to the Sanctuary on my own.

For several days I'd been trekking alone and, celebrating the freedom to go as far and as fast as I chose, I'd overdone it. The days had been long and tough with lots of altitude gain—but, feeling fit and acclimatized, I'd relished the challenge each trail presented. Once in the Sanctuary, that immense circle of peaks and glaciers, beginning with Hiunchuli and ending with Machhapuchhre, had justified the diversion. Annapurna's impressive south face was all and more than I'd expected; Singu Chuli and Tharpu Chuli were graceful; Gangapurna looked very different from when I'd last gazed upon it from the far side of the range. Machhapuchhre, however, was somehow less elegant than when seen from the approach to the Modi Khola's gorge, for the icy lodge at Annapurna Base Camp seemed to look down on that tail-like summit, despite it being almost 23,000 feet high.

The previous night, on my way out of the Sanctuary, I'd had to sleep on a lodge table as all the beds were taken. It was not the most restful of nights, so I blamed that for my weariness as, many hours later, I stepped onto the suspension bridge at the lower end of the gorge and felt all my energy draining away. I paused halfway across, held onto the steel cable, and looked into the Chhomrong Khola. Carrying the melt of a clutch of Himalayan glaciers and snowfields, the river swirled in pools and eddies, and crashed among boulders with a pulsating rhythm. My head spun; I felt giddy and weak.

Across the bridge the buildings of Chhomrong climbed an endless stairway of broad stone steps. On this day those steps were more like a vertical ladder reaching to the clouds, and it took every last ounce of energy to mount them.

Just below the lodge in which I'd stayed on the way in to the Sanctuary, I could go no further. My strength had gone, I was lathered in sweat and my legs had turned to jelly. So I crawled onto the slab-topped wall beside the steps and, using my rucksack for a pillow, stretched out—and in moments was fast asleep. Dead to the world.

I've no idea how long I lay there, but I was brought slowly back to life by a Nepali voice. "Old man tired?"

Through half-opened eyes I could see a lad of about fifteen peering down at me with obvious concern. A woman I took to be his mother stood to one side, and when our eyes met, she gave a smile of understanding.

"Old man *very* tired," I told him. There was no point denying it. I was exhausted.

"Which lodge you?" asked the lad as I raised myself on one elbow.

"That one," I said, pointing to a white building not fifty paces away. Only fifty paces, but they were all uphill. It could have been the north face of the Eiger.

The lad took my rucksack off the wall and hung it over one shoulder. He then chased up the steps while his mother walked slowly with me. One step at a time. For the old man was very tired.

SONG OF THE HIDDEN LAND

In 1995 I organized a trek across Dolpo for a group of friends. It proved to be one of the most exciting journeys I'd ever made, and many years later it still haunts my dreams. Dolpo is unique—the landscape is other-worldly, Dolpo-pa culture is very different from that of other Himalayan races, and I remain fascinated by what I experienced there. And long before the trek was over I was forced to reassess many Western values that I'd previously accepted without question.

With valleys more than 13,000 feet above sea level, the hidden land of Dolpo is said to be one of the highest permanently inhabited regions on Earth. As it lies remote among dun-colored mountains on the northern side of the Himalayan Divide, just getting there can be an adventure in itself. There are no roads. Highways are confined to historic trails scored over a series of passes by generations of heavily-laden yaks or herds of long-horned goats carrying salt to the south or heading north with sacks of grain. Lammergeyer haunt the skies, their cross-like shadows rippling across the hillsides. When the barley harvest has stripped the fields, this uncompromising landscape is scoured by winds that chase dust-devils through valleys and round villages of squat, flat-roofed houses fashioned from the ancient stone of an unforgiving land, where every day is a challenge for those who live there.

On a late-autumn afternoon I sat beside a Dolpo river, listening to the timeless sound of stones being smoothed and polished in its shallow bed—the splash and swirl, the rush and rustle of water's repeated actions unchanged over the past few million years. A simple wooden bridge spanned the river, and half a mile downvalley prayer flags raised above the houses of a small village beat a distant rhythm of reverence. Then human voices added to the sounds of river and wind-thrashed cloth, and, turning my head, I saw four women waltzing down the trail spinning yak wool on simple bobbins. They were singing, singing a curious melody, their faces alive with humor, and as they stepped onto the bridge each one in turn twirled in a wild dance, arms held high, bobbins shaking.

Once across the bridge they almost collapsed, breathless with laughter. Then they pulled themselves together and resumed their journey towards the village of Tok-khyu, singing once more. The wind caught their song and played with it.

Why so joyful in this harsh climate, this high-altitude desert devoid of comfort and ease? These women were going home to drafty houses, thinly furnished with yak- or goat-hair rugs, to sit by a yak-dung fire whose acrid smoke would fill every crevice in the room. they'd cook over that fire and eat the same meal twice a day every day of their lives. When their clothes wore out, they'd have to make more. They would never know a shop; never see a newspaper or a book other than the manuscript blocks they could not read in the village *gompa*. They'd never go to the cinema, watch television or listen to the radio. Many of their children would die in infancy; old age and prosperity is for those from a more benevolent climate. To my Western eyes theirs was a life of privation and austerity.

Yet they sang with unadulterated joy. A song of the hidden land.

LOST

From the final pass of our crossing of Dolpo, my Sherpa friend Kirken and I had caught sight of the great block of snow and ice that is Saipal, a 23,000 foot peak in the far west of Nepal. That vision inspired a dream, and in the spring of 1997, with five of his lads acting as porters, Kirken and I traveled as far west as you can go in Nepal, visited the base of Api, then worked our way eastwards to Saipal and beyond. This epic journey was made the more interesting as our map failed us in the early days of the journey. I learned then what it is to be truly lost.

As snowfall thickened and the afternoon light faded, Kirken called me back. "Too dangerous to continue," he said. "We find some place to camp."

So we backtracked a short way along the ridge until Pemba, I think it was, indicated that we could dig a couple of ledges just below the crest. An hour later the two tents were up, and the seven of us huddled inside and dreamed of brighter days.

It snowed all night, and although it eased when day broke, visibility was down to a few feet. None of this concerned the five Sherpas who had opted to come with Kirken and me to act as porters and to share our traverse of the far west. Their laughter echoed among the clouds, and if anything could bring on the sunshine, it would be their unfailing good humor.

When at last the cloud lifted, there was clearly no onward progress to be made along the ridge, so we scanned instead the south flank of the mountain which fell into an unknown valley. Unknown, yes, but everything was unknown to us, for we had already lost faith in the map, and I figured that if we were going to be lost, we might as well make a meal of it. So the map remained at the bottom of my rucksack, and each morning would begin by checking the compass with the aim of heading as best we could towards the east. Sometimes a big mountain would get in the way. But that merely added to the fun. And the confusion. We'd make a detour to the south until it was possible to cross a ridge, then head north to regain the suspected line of our eastward traverse. Being lost—I mean, totally lost—was the mark of our journey. Today was no exception.

Maila went in search of a way off the ridge, and eventually returned wearing a wide grin and a furrowed brow. Like meeting a barking dog with a wagging tail, I wasn't sure which expression to trust. Kirken interpreted. "He says it *looks* possible. If we are lucky. And very careful."

That descent is one I am heartily thankful never to have to face again, for I don't think any of us escaped without a few choice cuts or bruises. But several hours later we were down, hundreds of feet below the ridge, and after licking our wounds we trudged through rough little meadows and followed what appeared to be a faint trail leading to a confluence of valleys. Winter had been left behind. Here trees were flush with blossom, tiny flowers starred the meadows and, perched like nests among crags, between converging streams we spied five houses.

Settling ourselves beside the main stream Dorje lit a fire and began to prepare a meal while we waited for the approach of locals.

We didn't have long to wait, for two old men appeared in homespun tunics and trousers greasy with age and lack of soap. We shared with them our *daal bhat* and drank ginger tea; then, squatting on his hunkers, Kirken began to quiz them in an attempt to build an oral map.

What was the name of their village?

They gave it, although without a meaningful map it meant nothing to us.

What was the name of the river? A response was offered, but again the information meant nothing to us.

Where does the valley go? (This was important.) The two old men looked at one another, frowned, then gave a shrug of their shoulders. Where to? Their expression was one of complete bewilderment—why would anyone want to know such a thing?

One of the old men babbled something helpful, though. The gist of it was—if you go downstream for one day, you will come to another village.

That was the extent of their world; a day's walk downvalley. If they knew no more than that, we were well and truly lost. But there's freedom in not knowing where you are, and that was cause for celebration.

MOUNTAINEERS OF THE FUTURE

*Phortse is a typical Sherpa village built on a slope of farmland
facing southwest. Like so many Khumbu villages it is crowded by
huge mountains, but being off the main Everest trail it is much
less busy, and therefore more conservative, than the better-known
settlements between Namche and Pheriche. Since my first visit in
1993, whenever I've been in the area I've opted to spend a night or
two there.*

A hurricane lamp made the soft puttering sound of a contented
kitten, its orange glow too weak to reach the far end of the room
where adult members of the family sat. Their voices droned in lazy,
end-of-the-day fashion, their conversation broken by long minutes
of silence or interrupted by the chesty cough and catarrhal snort
of those whose lives have been spent in houses without chimneys.

It was a long room, a family room whose windows by day
looked out over dusty fields and along the depths of the Khumbu
valley. But it was dark now, and only by an effort of concentration
could pinpricks of starlight be detected through the dingy glass.
The opposite wall was lined with old expedition boxes that, when
opened, showed an assortment of hand-made rugs. Above them
wooden cupboards held bottles of Star beer, Fanta and Coke—the
only signs that the house was also used as a trekkers' lodge. First
and foremost it was a Sherpa home, with a distinct and powerful
ambience.

Tacked on the side of one of the cupboards, photographs showed
family members on mountaineering expeditions—men with red
down jackets posing with Western climbers; Sherpas with exposed
teeth like piano keys; young men with arms held aloft in celebration of a summit reached; others squatting in front of dome tents.

One had a note underneath announcing that the man in the photo had reached the summit of Everest three years earlier. Tonight I was living among a people whose lives swing on a pendulum from pragmatic tillers of soil to the deadly, dangerous world of high-altitude portering. One life revolved around the fertility of fields that would be frozen for several long weeks of winter; the other risked frostbite and death to boost the ego of others.

Mountaineers of the future played around me—three young children and a baby held in a sling over a five-year-old's shoulder. Typically their faces were grimed with dirt and gluey from ever-running noses, but beneath the crust red cheeks glowed and eyes flashed with the immediacy of childhood joy. In another minute they could be spraying tears, but for now, this moment in time was all that mattered. The game consumed all thought, all of life itself. But suddenly a new idea sprang to a little boy's mind, and he scuttled to one of the expedition boxes, rummaged in it and emerged with a yak bell that made a dull "clonk" when shaken. The bell was fixed to a loop of rope, and the child wound it round and round until he was no longer in danger of tripping over. Transformed, the child became a yak; his fingers were horns, and he stomped to and fro, snorting.

A tiny girl, sister to the yak, lost interest and wandered to the adult end of the room, scuffing her bare feet. Without interrupting her parents, she absently began to sing in a piping voice that scratched at my heart. In a flash the years flew by and I was in the garden at home where my eldest daughter, then only three or four, was singing beneath a wild cherry tree full of blossom, singing to the sunbeams.

It was impossible to concentrate on my journal, for I was desperate to miss nothing. This Phortse evening had funneled the life of mountain Nepal into a glass jar of experience. I wished for nothing to be left out, for I knew that in years to come the jar would be held up to the light and its contents looked at many times. So

I sat and absorbed the minutes that flowed with a rhythm of their own into wholesome hours.

The little girl who sang grew tired. Without being instructed to, she drifted (it was not a walk, for she seemed almost to float across the room) to the deep-cushioned bench seat next to where I sat. And there, with no hint of embarrassment, she wearily removed her clothes, dropped them in a rumpled heap on the floor, clambered onto the bench beside me, pulled a rug over her little body, and in moments was asleep.

TO THE ENDS OF THE EARTH

Since my first visit to the Himalaya, Kangchenjunga has drawn me back several times, and in 2005 I was offered the chance to lead a trek towards that huge mountain via the Singalila Ridge, and then, in Sikkim, up to the Goecha La. With near-perfect conditions practically every day, the Singalila Ridge provided the most exquisite views of the world's third highest mountain—and much more besides.

The Singalila Ridge is born among ice-crusted outliers of the Kangchenjunga massif and marks the border between northeast Nepal and the remote Indian region of Sikkim. It then stretches far to the south beyond Sikkim to flank the hill country of West Bengal in view of the tea gardens of Darjeeling.

Each day of our trek along that ridge began with a view from our tent of sunrise blushing Kangchenjunga, the world's third highest peak, and ended with the same great mountain turning bronze before night took over. It was hard to believe that anything could improve those scenes of dramatic beauty, but on the fifth day we took a path out of the village of Sabarkum, passed a *chorten* sprouting prayer flags, dodged among pink-barked rhododendron trees long out of bloom, and came to an open section of ridge. The tinkling of bells and chatter of Sherpas warned that our mules were coming, but as there was room for them to pass I continued to dawdle, eyes darting this way and that in search of autumn flowers.

Our path brought us to the top of a short rise, and as one we all stopped in our tracks—mules and Sherpas too—as the ridge fell before us into a scoop of valley, leaving no higher land between us and the huge arctic wall of the Himalayan giants.

Still several days' walk ahead, Kangchenjunga stood before us. It looked immense—as indeed it is. Beside it to the west rose Jannu, shapely, handsome, and deeply impressive. Beyond that, further away, was Makalu, the world's fourth highest mountain, and maybe sixty miles beyond that, beyond the whaleback of Chamlang and Baruntse, rose Lhotse and Everest. The ragged Himalayan line continued on and on out to the far west, gradually narrowing to a vague point where earth finally blended into sky.

East of Kangchenjunga stood the mountains of Sikkim, among which we'd soon be trekking. A few Tibetan peaks intruded, but further on Chomolhari crested the border of Bhutan, while more and more crowded peaks stretched the horizon out to the distant east. It was difficult to comprehend just how far we could see, but the light was pure and sparkling, the atmosphere having been laundered by the monsoon rains, and our vision was unimpaired, uninterrupted. A white line, now wafer thin until it too became blurred against the sky, eventually shrank that mountain wall to oblivion. From west to east the curve of the Earth was a reality rarely seen. It stretched for hundreds of miles.

As we stood there transfixed by the vastness of the scene, a golden eagle drifted out of the valley, rode the thermals on outstretched wings, then hovered directly above us so that we could see all the underwing markings and hear the rippling breeze through its feathers. And even the Sherpas fell silent.

A SHADOW TO CHERI GOMPA

The name "Bhutan" has a mystical ring about it. Secluded among the Himalaya immediately to the east of Sikkim, it's about the same size as Switzerland, but with a population of considerably less than a million. Traditional values are an obvious sign of its long isolation from outside influence, and the gentle elegance and hospitable nature of its people, together with exquisite buildings and beautiful scenery, have created an image of Shangri La among the more romantic visitors to this Land of the Thunder Dragon. In 2009 I had the privilege of leading a cultural tour there, during which we drifted from one medieval dzong to another, and from monastery to monastery set among the wooded middle hills.

Draining the high country of northwest Bhutan, the Thimpu Chhu is a vigorous river, surging through the valley with a rumble of shifting rocks that relegates birdsong to the realms of imagination. I could see the birds chatting to one another on branches overhead where, dressed in sober black plumage, a soloist would suddenly throw back his head and with beak opened wide warble a love song unheard down by the water. Suddenly a frenzy of half a dozen birds erupted from a curtain of leaves and swept away into the sunlight, leaving me with a flutter of prayer flags strung across the *chhu*. Enriched by the blessings I crossed the handsome covered bridge and began the climb to Cheri Gompa, the 450-year-old monastery built way up on the hillside.

My group had gone ahead with Kinley, our Bhutanese guide, which granted me the luxury of a solitary approach. It was a morning to savor, and as I gained height the river lost its voice and was replaced by the birdsong denied earlier. Birdsong, the busy fever of insects, and the odd slap of leather on stone were all that disturbed the peace.

Some time later I had a feeling that I was not alone. Pausing on a bend in the trail I turned to discover a few paces behind me a short, elderly woman with cropped gray hair and wrinkles etched into her broad face. She stopped too and stood motionless, with arms limp by her sides, her eyes cast shyly down at her feet. Until, that is, I spoke: "Hello," I said. "Kuzo zangpo la!" She looked up then, and a smile beamed back at me. She did not reply, but instead wavered her head from side to side, which I took to be her response.

Clothed from neck to ankle in a traditional *kira*, this grandmotherly figure epitomized the grace, elegance, and quiet dignity of the Bhutanese people it had been my privilege to meet in the last few days, and I was immediately warmed by her presence. The bright red *kira* had a horizontal pattern and large white sleeve cuffs. A ceremonial scarf hung across her shoulders, and two rows of cream-colored beads stood out against the red; the right thumb fed a rosary against the palm of her hand. Behind her stretched the wooded middle hills of this Himalayan kingdom; a very different landscape from those I had explored elsewhere in the Himalaya—but, like the woman standing before me, it had taken no time at all to win me over.

I took a step backward and indicated she should pass, but she remained firmly where she stood. We exchanged smiles, and when I resumed the walk up the steepening trail, I was aware that she was walking just behind me once more, step for step all the way. And when I stopped again, several minutes later, she stopped too. We smiled at one another, and although no more words passed between us, we developed an understanding. She became my shadow on the trail.

Passing below lengthy strings of prayer flags that stretched from tree to tree across the hillside, we reached the *gompa* a moment or two behind my group, and I suddenly realized that my shadow had slipped past me and was almost floating across the paved square. The cloth that covered a doorway moved slightly, and the woman in the bright red *kira* disappeared from view.

Cheri Gompa rose in tiers against the hillside—sturdy white stone, with brown timber-framed windows and projecting eaves. Monks in claret robes, venerable laymen and women too, spun the hundreds of prayer wheels that adorned the outer walls, and we in turn made our *kora* behind them. At the main entrance we removed our boots, then Kinley led us inside, where a *puja* was taking place. We slid to the floor and sat entranced.

Rows of monks both young and old electrified the air with their chanting, bodies swaying to and fro under the hypnotic power of prayer. Deep growling voices boomed around the shaven heads of those seated in front, silver bells rang, *puja* sticks tapped out a rhythm, brass cymbals clashed, then long clarinet-like trumpets were raised and the whole building trembled at the tuneless eruption of sound. Then silence.

In the place of honor sat an old man wearing a pair of wire-rimmed spectacles perched upon his nose. Kinley whispered that he was the former head lama of Bhutan, now 97 years old. He looked tired but not exactly frail, and I wondered how he'd managed to climb the hillside to reach this revered site. Later we saw the wooden chair, set on a stretcher-like contraption, on which he'd been carried by his acolytes. Bent low with arthritis, when he stood he leaned on a stick for support, yet his authority was palpable. Here was a man held in respect by all in attendance; a man to whom each one present would defer and look for spiritual guidance. His great age only added weight to the dignity of his former position.

And when the *puja* was over, the old man was helped down the steps, where he then stood and, one by one, gave each of us a blessing. Overhead the strings of colored prayer flags caught the breeze, and a flurry of birds raced by. Far off the mountains of Bhutan tossed stray clouds. And the heavens sang.

BALLAST

Getting to and away from the mountains is often the most stressful part of any Himalayan trek or expedition. Our journey to the farthest west of Nepal in 1997 had taken many days and nights of travel by overcrowded bus and truck, so we considered ourselves extremely lucky at the end of our long traverse to get seats on a small plane within 24 hours of reaching our destination. But we hadn't considered the possibility of disruption by bad weather . . . or its consequences.

Our flight to Nepalgunj, on the border with India, should have taken no more than about forty minutes. Strapped in my seat I was wracked by a helter-skelter of emotions. One of the most exciting and demanding of expeditions was now over, and I regretted the fact that there would be no more adventures—at least for a few months. On the other hand I was now starting the long journey home; home to wife, family, and friends whom I'd not seen for what seemed half a lifetime. I longed to be with them right now—but I knew I'd miss the chatter of Dorje, Pemba, Maila, and Co; sharing stories and dreams with Kirken; the sound of creaking *dokos*; the epic laughter round a campfire. But it would be heaven to lie in a bath, to wear clean clothes, to sit at a table and eat a meal with vegetables straight from the garden—not to mention the luxury of being able to drink water straight from the tap . . . The loud throbbing of the plane's engines defied conversation, and I was aware of Kirken's head nodding with sleep. Dorje's was pressed against his window, mesmerized by the land far below that tumbled from mountains to foothills, brown and hazy, and was sliced by a river in whose shallows buffalo stood—no larger than shiny black beetles.

Then the plane tilted to the right, the earth slid away, and all I could see was sky before the pilot leveled the wings once more. Now we were heading in another direction. Before we'd been aiming due south. Now we were heading northwest, and foothills were growing to middle hills, beyond which a line of snow peaks formed a horizon that should have been low, dull, featureless—and lying to the south. Where were we going?

Kirken woke. He rubbed his eyes, peered out of his window, then turned to me and gestured—where are we going? I shrugged. Who knows?

There was no-one to ask. This was no international airline with smartly dressed cabin staff; there was no button to press to summon a steward. In our cramped twelve-seater we had a clear view of the pilot and co-pilot—so we hadn't been hijacked. But why had we changed course? And where were we going?

We lost altitude, hopped across low ridges and scoured the land below. Then the co-pilot pointed at something, the pilot adjusted his speed, and moments later we were bumping across a meadow with no buildings in sight.

When at last we stopped and the engines were silenced, the pilot turned in his seat to explain. Apparently he had received a radio message to say that Nepalgunj was being hit by a severe storm and it would not be safe to attempt a landing there until the storm had moved on. "We'll just wait here," he said, "until I receive an okay. It could be an hour or so. Get out, stretch your legs, make your-selves comfortable." His co-pilot came through the cabin, opened the door, released the steps and let us out.

Kirken was soon stretched out asleep on the grass. The other five lads who had acted as our porters for the past weeks were in a huddled group playing cards. I sat nearby with my back to a rock and gazed south at a tide of evil cloud slowly drifting our way. The storm was on the move.

There was no sign of pilot or co-pilot. Where had they gone? There was no village evident, just unused pastureland and a few large boulders, with hills to the north that obscured the mountains we'd spent weeks traversing.

The bruised cloud stretched across the sky. It swallowed the sun, cast a wash of shadow over the land, and moved steadily towards us. A hot wind rippled the grass. Birds fell silent.

Suddenly the pilot ran across the grass shouting, "In the plane, quick!" I woke Kirken, and all seven of us ran to the tiny aircraft, climbed aboard and tightened the seat belts, assuming we would take off, fly away from the approaching storm and make a devious flight to Nepalgunj. Not so. The pilot slammed the door from outside and secured it, and moments later we could see him running away with the co-pilot.

Kirken, the lads, and I were left alone in the plane, strapped into our seats as the first rush of wind hit. The plane rocked, then was hit again. Suddenly lightning ripped across the sky and rain fell in a monsoon-like downpour. Again and again the aircraft shook under the onslaught; we were buffeted and bullied while rain streaked the windows and misted the land outside. The plane shuddered and rocked; it was the nearest I've come to being air sick, although we were still on the ground.

The storm lasted about twenty minutes, but it seemed much longer. The rain eased, then stopped completely. The wind died, the tide of cloud moved further north and the sun came out again. All around the plane grass steamed and the distant hills quivered.

Unabashed, the pilot and co-pilot reappeared. Where they'd been we never did discover, but they were dry, so they must have found shelter somewhere.

Both climbed into the cockpit, and before he strapped himself in the pilot turned to us and said, "Okay, we can go now. Everyone happy?"

It was then that we understood. To prevent the plane from being blown over by the wind, the pilot had used Kirken, the lads, and me as human ballast.

The swine!

SAVING TSEWAN

In more than fifty years of mountain activity I've been extremely fortunate to be involved in very few accidents or emergencies. On trek with a group of friends in the Everest region in 2004, one such emergency happened in what turned out to be a rather fortunate location—anywhere else on our route and the consequences would have been very different.

Ice coated the stream in the ablation valley beside the Khumbu glacier, but as we lost height, with our backs to Pumori, frost flowers were replaced by gentians, and by mid-morning the sun's warmth—even in November—was enough to release the stream and send it chortling free. Out of the wind we stopped at a tea-house in Dughla, with the neighboring peaks of Taboche and Cholatse looking down on us. We sat at a table in the sunshine, drank lemon tea, and nibbled a few biscuits, then set off again, crossing the bridge, and taking the uppermost trail that cuts along the old moraine shelf below Pokalde and leads directly to Dingboche.

Most of the group had gone ahead, while I was walking with Kirken and his brother-in-law Tsewan, discussing plans for the next few days of our trek. Tsewan was the oldest, strongest, and most agile of our crew. A quiet man in his forties, he'd been to 27,000 feet on Everest, and had climbed Manaslu and several other major peaks, but seldom spoke of his experiences unless pressed. On this trek he was Kirken's right-hand man, and I knew we were lucky to have him with us.

Suddenly, and without any prior warning, he clutched his stomach and started to vomit. He didn't lose much food, but coughed and choked for what seemed like a few minutes, with sweat running down his face. Kirken guided him to a rock and encouraged him to sit. I waited at a discreet distance until he felt better, assuming it was something he'd eaten. The incident passed, but although he was a little shaky on his feet for a moment, he refused to let Kirken take his rucksack and hurried on ahead. I imagine he was embarrassed by a sign of what he may have considered weakness, and preferred to be alone for a while.

It was a scenic trail, with graceful Ama Dablam directly in front but almost a day's walk away, Taboche and Cholatse above to the right, and a view back towards the Cho La, which we'd crossed on our way from Gokyo to Kala Pattar. A string of laden yaks came lumbering towards us, clouds of dust being stirred by their hooves, and steam snorting from their nostrils as they passed.

Kirken and I were lost in our own thoughts, drifting through one of the world's most exciting landscapes, relaxed now with the toughest stages of the trek behind us. The big moraine wall that separates Pheriche from Dingboche was growing in stature as we drew near; beyond that stretched the valley of the Imja Khola—the way to Island Peak. But the main valley of the Khumbu curved to the right directly below Ama Dablam, and that was where we'd be going in a couple of days' time. Perhaps tomorrow we could trek to Chhukung . . . I was aware of a group of figures ahead. As they were huddled together my first thought was that our cook, Pasang, had sent one of the Sherpas to meet us with a kettle of juice. But as we drew nearer it became clear that this was not the case. Someone was on the ground.

It was Tsewan, surrounded by porters and four of my group. "What's happened?" I asked.

"We don't know; he was found like this. He's out for the count."

I checked his pulse. It was erratic, his skin clammy. He opened an eye and groaned, clutching his stomach once more. He tried to sit up, but fell back again, face contorted with pain, hands pressed tightly into his stomach. "He needs medical help," I told Kirken. "But we're in luck. The trekkers' aid post is just below in Pheriche; we must get him to the doctor."

"I will carry," said Kirken. "You run to the aid post."

Turning to the members of my group, I asked them to help Kirken, then took off, swooping down the slope towards Pheriche's rooftops. It was steep, but several paths had been created, and the urgency of the situation made me reckless.

By the time I reached the health post I was seriously out of breath and coughing badly. "You've got a cough," said the doctor, and held out his hand. "I'm Mike."

"Thanks," I wheezed. "But it's not me I'm concerned about. It's one of my Sherpas . . . he's in trouble up on the hill."

"Okay, tell me slowly what seems to be the problem." As I was describing what had happened we walked outside, where we heard shouting and looked up to find Tsewan rushing down the hill, with Kirken and the others right behind him. Momentum kept him running until he reached the foot of the slope, where he then collapsed at our feet.

Mike, the English volunteer doctor, took over along with his female colleague. Tsewan was lifted into the surgery, while Kirken and I hovered outside the door. Nearby, a tall stainless steel pyramid recalled the names of Everest summiteers and those who had lost their lives on the mountain. I remembered my promise to photograph it for a friend at home, whose son was the sculptor who created it. Now did not seem the right time for photography.

Five minutes later we were called in. Tsewan had an oxygen mask over his face, wires were attached to his chest, and his heart was being monitored by the female doctor. "He's had a heart attack," said Mike. "God knows how he made it down here. We need to get him to hospital. And quick."

The next few minutes were a blur of activity and decision making. Before we could call for a helicopter, the cost of callout had to be guaranteed. No good saying you have insurance; up here you need cash or a credit card. At least $3,000, we were told. John came up trumps. "Use my card," he said, and handed it over.

Through the crackling of static, a call was sent to Kathmandu. Kirken would fly with Tsewan, arrange hospitalization, make all the necessary arrangements for his meals, sort out payment for his care, and make contact with his family, who were in Solu region.

While Tsewan was fighting for his life, another emergency was also taking place. A porter working for a group heading for Island Peak was being brought down with a suspected perforated ulcer. Carried on a homemade stretcher, he was taken into a side-room for diagnosis. This revealed that he too needed to be airlifted out.

"He needs an operation as soon as possible," said Mike. "It's a good thing a helicopter's on its way. I assume it's okay for him to go with your man?"

"Of course."

The helicopter arrived, and there was no shortage of volunteers to carry the two patients on their stretchers. Mike was giving instructions to the pilot as Kirken gave me a bear hug, then started to climb aboard. But the co-pilot would have none of it. "No room," he was saying. "We're at the top of our weight limit for this altitude," and he shoved him away.

My long-time Sherpa friend looked distraught and shouted against the deafening noise as I pulled him away. "I should be with Tsewan," he cried, but the helicopter door was closed, and the engine noise rose to new levels as we ducked our heads and ran towards the health post. We stopped then to watch as the machine lifted hesitantly from the ground, tail raised, nose pointing down, then flew low along the valley before rising and turning to the south, growing smaller until it was no more than a ladybird disappearing through an avenue of lofty mountains.

Kirken's eyes were misty, and his lips mumbled an old Buddhist prayer. Then he ran for the satellite phone.

....

This story has a mixed ending. Initially Kirken managed to contact a family member in Kathmandu, who immediately rushed to the airport and transferred Tsewan to hospital, where he took care of the cost of the patient's treatment and food until Kirken was back in town. The day before we flew back to the UK we met Tsewan at Kirken's house. He was pale and weak, but thankful to be alive. Sadly, despite being advised against a return to high altitudes, a year later Tsewan was trekking in the Annapurnas (he knew no other way to earn a living), where he had another massive heart attack and died before medical help could reach him.

WITH THE AID OF A HEARSE

As I travel through the "unboundaried kingdom of the mind" during sleepless nights, images of Manaslu and the snowy Larkya La often feature. On two memorable occasions I'd been trekking there, and with so many of Nepal's once-remote valleys now being penetrated by dirt roads, I had a yearning to tackle the Manaslu Circuit once more before the landscape was irrevocably scarred by bulldozer. But it was 2009, my lungs were wrecked, and I wondered whether I still had the puff to make it. However, Kirken had a solution . . . With damaged lungs it was obvious that altitude would now be a major struggle for me, but I was determined to go as high as I could and, being aware that this might be my last major Himalayan trek, wanted to make the most of it. The Manaslu Circuit had always been special, and Kirken, who'd trekked that route with me in the past, not just as sirdar *but as a friend, knew the score. "Don't worry," he tried to reassure me. "If you can get to Samdo, I'll find you a hearse."*

"A hearse?" I cried. "I might have trouble breathing at 14,000 feet, but I have no intention of dying there. In any case, what's the use of a hearse in a land without roads?"

"A hearse," he said, "to ride to the pass."

I laughed, then. "You mean a horse!"

"Horse? Hearse? Same thing—yes?"

As ever the trek along the valley of the Buri Gandaki was full of beauty, full of interest. The trail through the gorge allowed brief glimpses of snow peaks, and its walls showered the most exquisite waterfalls; the sound of rockfall followed our group for half a day beyond Labubesi; white-faced monkeys watched from trees as we passed. A succession of makeshift bridges shook and shuddered as we crossed foaming tributaries. Every half-hour rewarded with a fresh experience.

Passing the massive *kani* at Lhogaon, with its heart-stopping view of Manaslu, Kirken found a local man going our way leading a horse. Moments later he insisted I ride as far as our next camp. "See how you like," he grinned.

I'd not been on a horse for forty-odd years, yet I took to it straightaway. But the wooden saddle made its mark, and by the time we'd reached Syala an hour or so later I swore I'd never sit down again. Both buttocks were raw.

Two days later the slope that led to Samdo, our highest village, had me gasping for breath. Not far from our tents the Tibetan refugees, who'd built the village from scratch, were beating harvested barley with long bamboo flails. Clouds of chaff floated above walled enclosures, while black-haired yaks scuffed the bare fields. In every direction huge mountains wearing their armour of ice and snow glistened in the Himalayan sunlight. Samdo never failed to excite, and I was thankful to be back.

"I've found you a hearse," said Kirken. "Two days to Larkya La. Be good, eh?"

He introduced me to the woman who owned the short-legged Tibetan pony. A handsome woman with high cheekbones and the horny hands of someone used to hard physical work, she looked me in the eyes and said something incomprehensible. She was probably thinking, "Poor old man. It'll be a miracle if he makes it to the pass."

Anticipating an uncomfortable ride, large pads of Compeed were stuck to each buttock and a sit-mat stuffed down my trousers, yet within two minutes the sit-mat had ridden up my back and I could feel every movement of the horse beneath me. Even so, it was an exhilarating ride. In places the trail was so narrow that my right leg rubbed against rocks, while my left foot was suspended above a steep slope that swept hundreds of feet to a stream; but on coming to a place where a landslide had destroyed the trail I gingerly walked across, while the Samdo woman led the horse. Off to my left a secret half-hidden, glacier-cut valley suggested a wonderland I'd never explore. But I could dream.

We camped 2,000 feet higher than Samdo, and long before dawn next day started for the pass. Apart from the crunching of boots on frozen snow, the only sound came from the tinkling of bells fitted to my saddle. The beaming lights of headtorches turned to pinpricks as we drew away from the group. Although I knew I'd never make it on foot, I would love to have been with them, puffing towards the pass once more in the raw, cold morning. Instead, the horse carried me ever higher, plodding up the trough of snow-covered moraine, its breath snorting in clouds of steam as day made its welcome appearance and an unnamed mountain north of the pass turned gold before my eyes.

The snow softened. Deep drifts confused the way, and my mount floundered. So I called a halt, slid from the saddle, paid the woman, thanked her and the horse with real gratitude, and watched as they turned for home, slithering downhill.

With perhaps 500 vertical feet to climb the 17,100 foot pass, I plunged a foot into the snow, gasped for breath, then tried another. Then another. My chest heaved as my lungs felt tight and far too small for the job they were called upon to do. But slow and steady progress was made, and at last I staggered onto the Larkya La, where colored prayer flags exercised the wind. A short walk to the west I knew the Annapurnas would come into view, as well as Himlung Himal and Cheo Himal on the Tibetan border, their long glacier ribbons spilling down to Bimtang among stripes of moraine. I'd see them again, after all. Once would have been cause for celebration, but this would be my third time. That it would also be my last was not worth thinking about.

On the frost-glistening snow of the Larkya La I was thankful for "now," for this moment in time. Sinking among a pile of rocks out of the wind, I gave up a prayer of gratitude and waited for Kirken, the porters, Sherpas, my wife and friends with working lungs to join me.

Sometimes you reach a heaven on earth and recognize it. With the aid of a hearse, I'd made it to mine.

PASA CHAUR

Days spent among the high mountains are almost always rewarding, and once they've been left behind it's easy to forget the raw cold and hours of discomfort, leaving only scenic highlights or dramatic moments to represent truth. Time spent in the foothills is often glossed over. But on a journey such as our circuit of Manaslu in 2009, the humid rice-growing country towards the end of our trek was not only vibrant with activity as the crops were being harvested, but it produced an unforgettable meeting with a village of smiles and flowers.

Our days in the high mountains were over and, passing through the middle hills, our descent to the steamy foothills was a shock to the system. Although it was November, and a backward glance showed 26,000 foot peaks of the Annapurna and Manaslu Himals, the temperature hovered between 85° and 90°. Humidity was high, and sweat dripped from us. The day's trek had been a long one and now, late in the afternoon and in need of a rest, we came to the outskirts of a small village where we spied a patch of uncultivated land large enough to accommodate our tents. A woman at a nearby house agreed to our camping there, and while the Sherpas were erecting the tents, we were surrounded by local children. A book with photographs of the mountains appeared from a ruck sack, and the children became animated as they recognized some of the peaks, the names of the valleys and rivers.

Faces shone with smiles of familiarity.

Darkness fell. Pemba produced yet another filling meal, and after we'd eaten our camp was visited by the whole village—about 60 people in all; men, women, and children. They brought garlands of marigolds to hang round our necks. Ceremonial scarves were draped over our shoulders, scarlet powder sprinkled on each nose and forehead, and gifts of bananas were handed round.

A young man gave a speech of welcome, and when a lad began tapping a rhythm on a drum, two women got up to dance as the rest of the villagers broke into song. The dancers were graceful with every movement, shaming our clumsiness when we were enticed to dance with them. Moonlight threw shadows and picked out gleaming eyes and white teeth.

Dew was on the ground as we prepared to leave early next morning, each of us wearing the garlands again so that they could be cast into the first river we'd cross in order to carry goodwill downstream. A woman came out of her house and placed a *tikka* on each forehead; she put flowers in our hair and blessed us. Another pressed bougainvillea blossoms into our palms, and as we walked through the village everyone stood outside their homes with hands together in an attitude of prayer. "Namaste" hung in the air: "I salute the god within you."

The young man who'd given the speech of welcome last night accompanied us to the village boundary. There he shook each one by the hand and begged us not to forget him or his neighbors. "We will not forget you," he said, then explained that we were the first foreigners to pass through the village in more than 18 months. And as our trail took us up a slope and round a wooded spur out of sight, we could still hear the children calling "Namaste" and ullulating their farewell. There was not a dry eye among us.

Pasa Chaur is not marked on any map. It stands astride a trail that goes nowhere in particular. The people who live there are subsistence farmers leading simple lives of hard graft and uncertainty, but they displayed warm hearts, spontaneous friendship, generosity, and love. They asked for nothing but our friendship in return, and we were humbled by it.

Pasa Chaur. It may be forgotten by the map makers, but not by us.

OTHER WILD PLACES

A Kaleidoscope of Experience

C hoosing a freelance career is never taken lightly, for it involves turning one's back on regular employment, a guaranteed income, and a degree of stability—the comedy writer Frank Muir once referred to it as "self un-employment." But, given a certain amount of luck, hard work, and the ability to spot an opportunity, it does have its positive side, as a number of occasions have proved. With a readiness to grab a rucksack and go, I have followed work to an assortment of far-flung lands such as Norway, Spain, eastern Turkey, the Peruvian Andes, and the islands of Corsica, Madeira, and Tenerife. Tales from each of these recorded here came as the result of either a writing commission or researching routes for mountain holidays.

Norway, for example, had been on my list of "must visit" places for years. A vision of deep fjords penetrating into glacier-scoured mountains made the prospect of a visit irresistible, while a region of sun-bleached sierras behind Spain's Costa Blanca was completely unknown to me until I received a surprise call to go there on a press trip. An invitation to travel to Turkey to climb Mount Ararat was also totally unexpected, but rewarding, while adventures in Corsica and the Cordillera Blanca of Peru were made on behalf of two trekking companies.

This is just a small selection of stories brought up from the well of memory. Others from the Caucasus of Russia, from Poland's Tatra Mountains, the magical high-altitude desert of Ladakh, the Blue Mountains of Australia, and New Zealand's Southern Alps remain undisturbed—for now. But each visit was crowded with moments, the moments that make life special.

SUN AND SNOW ON THE SCENTED ISLE

Seen from the air, Corsica is a fretwork of bays cut from a dense block of granite that runs from one end of the island to the other. On closer inspection that granite block is broken into individual peaks and ridges, dotted with pools, slashed with waterfalls, and divided by fragrant valleys. In the early summer of 1987 I accompanied a group trekking along Corsica's spine, taking the opportunity to stray onto some of its loftiest summits.

Ice floes drifted in the lake trapped below the summit crags of Monte Rotondo, and large patches of snow spread against the base of the cirque wall. Despite being less than 8,000 feet above the Mediterranean, our bivouac among the rocks promised to be one of the coldest so far, and as the sun went down the water turned black as if to emphasize the fact. There was no wind. The cirque emptied of sound, and stars multiplied in a velvet sky.

Sleep was elusive, but I was comfortable enough as I lay there replaying our trek and climbs of the past few days on Corsica's granite backbone. We'd had a full complement of mist, rain, sleet, and hours of burning sun, and accepted whatever each day brought. Between dawn and dusk we'd walk and scramble and absorb the beauty of this scented isle until we were replete. Some nights we'd sleep in huts; more often than not we'd stretch out beneath the stars and be aware of the world spinning through space. As now.

We rose with the dawn and watched as the land below dispensed with shadow and took on a misty patina. Before colors could form, Corsica appeared as unfinished as a slowly cooling meteorite, but some way above us the tip of a rock pinnacle glowed like a blacksmith's fire.

With 1,000 feet to climb before we could stand on the summit, we were soon stumbling over snow-covered scree and boulders, then heading up a gully on rock that chilled fingers before it led onto a ridge beside the pinnacle that had now lost its glow. It was a splendid vantage point, but we did not linger to enjoy it, for the mountain's crown was not far off and we were eager to be there. So we stormed along the ridge and scrambled up the final rocks to emerge by a small but solid-looking *abri* tucked just below the summit itself.

All of Corsica, it seemed, lay before us. Monte Rotondo's reputation as the island's ultimate viewpoint was accepted as fact. Mountains and valleys stretched into the distance to north and south. All the major summits were gathered on a gray granite spine. Most were bare of snow, but the morning light painted individual features that gave character to some of the highest, many of which we'd climbed during these past few days. Plunging to right and left, deep valleys hid their secrets. Down there, we'd discovered the luxury of clear green pools, long cascades tipping over slabs, stands of Corsican pine with cyclamen at their base, the fragrance of wild thyme, and the thunder of bees transporting pollen from flower head to flower head. Corsica had spun a web of fascination, and we'd been caught in it.

I gazed out to the east. Beyond a ragged knot of mountains the sun lit upon curving bays of the Mediterranean. When I turned to the west, out there beyond another knot of mountains I spied more curving bays and the gleaming sea. By mid-morning topless sun-worshippers would no doubt be spread across the sand of those bays; it would be like gazing across rows of poached eggs. But up here on Monte Rotondo's summit, we'd keep our shirts on. We had more mountains to climb.

[NORWAY]

THE BLESSINGS OF BAD-WEATHER DAYS

In June 2003, when checking routes for a mountain walking holiday based in Voss, I was constantly frustrated either by heavy rain or by a deep covering of snow giving white-out conditions. None of this stopped me going out each day, and despite the frustrations I would discover something to lift my spirits.

Mjølfjell was silent, battened against the early summer downpour. The scattered village was deserted—no smoke rose from its chimneys; no curtain twitched as I passed. There was no sign of life anywhere. Rain bounced off the tarmac and swilled down the drains. Cloud tatters shredded in valley trees, and a cold breeze huffed along the river. It was the kind of day, as someone once remarked, when only a fool or a guidebook writer would venture out. As I was not researching a guidebook on this occasion, I guess that branded me a fool.

Undeterred, and clad in rain gear with umbrella arced against the weather, I splashed down the track to the river and crossed by a suspension bridge that swayed and bounced with the same drunken disorder I'd grown accustomed to in the Himalaya.

The path climbed a slope of twenty shades of green, twisting among bilberry, birch, juniper, alder, pine, dwarf azalea, and heather a long way from flowering. Off to my right waterfalls exploded, draining last winter's snow and the deluge of past days. The mountainside trembled beneath the weight of so much water, and wreaths of spray drifted with the wind.

A stairway of cascades drew me up to the first lake. Bulbous at its northern end, it tapered with projections of rock and moss pushing jetties out from the bank. Tiny islands wore miniature birches, while those that grew on the slack shoreline were either bent or broken by the treachery of past seasons. Avalanche debris told its own story. Yet somewhere out of the gloom a cuckoo sounded a reminder of brighter days than this.

Passing a *saeter* locked and shuttered for a few more weeks, I continued to pick my way over rock tips just above the water and made it to the end of the lake where the river-sliced flats were still banked high with snow. All further progress was barred by a river so wildly in spate that it would have been suicidal to attempt its crossing alone. Without regret I peered at the slope that rose into cloud, and, knowing that was where my planned route would have led if I had been foolish enough to be tempted, I turned away. Sufficient unto the day, I faced into the rain and twenty minutes later sought shelter beneath the *saeter*'s out-house to make fresh plans.

For two hours I crouched there alongside the remnants of a sheep left by some scavenging animal for another day. I ate my bread rolls, nibbled chocolate, and waited for the rain to ease. It did. Then stopped completely.

Breaking free I stretched stiff limbs, shook the umbrella, and began to amble downvalley. The train back to base was not due for another four hours, and I could make it to the station in one, if I hurried. But this was not a hurrying day. Forty years ago (maybe more) I'd discovered a truth—bad-weather days repay the senses.

So that hour-long retreat downvalley consumed three and a bit. Had the sun been out I doubt if I'd have appreciated the valley as much as I did. My memories would have been mostly visual and on a larger scale. They'd have been dominated by mountains, reflections in lakes and the sparkle of cascades.

Instead I noticed other things—smaller, more intimate features of this valley in transition from winter to summer. I noticed the sandwich of quartz trapped in a boulder; tiny plants—some in bud, some daring to open in flower. There were intricate lichens and mosses, the tattered bark of a dwarf silver birch with its rain-polished sheen, and miniature cup-like leaves that suckered onto rocks in a tiny dell of stone and bush. There were toy-sized ferns with fronds the length of a fingernail and diminutive forests of mare's tail, remnants of a prehistoric age. My eyes focused upon a Lilliputian world.

I strayed this way and that with time my ally, gently pressing fingers into the soft, spongy lichens that reminded me of gray-green coral, and when I found a fist-sized piece about to drift away in the wind, I lifted it to my face and drew in its delicate chipped-rock fragrance. Everything in nature has its own bouquet, so I went adventuring with olfactory observations as rewarding as those of sight, sound, and touch. Alone in this wild valley there were none to witness my actions; none to condemn gray-haired folly.

Excitement won the day. A new flower daring to expose itself to the changing light, a plant soft as silk, the juicy fleshiness of a leaf with raindrops still attached, the scent of damp juniper contrasting that of an acidic bog. And as I faltered and floundered, a stonechat chittered, willow warblers and bramblings came to visit, the cuckoo once more echoed in the mist, and a dipper bobbed on a half-submerged rock in midstream. Having grown deaf to the river's thunder, I became aware instead of softer sounds. Around me birdsong proclaimed territorial limits or advertised for a mate.

But it was the lichens that captured my imagination. Unlike any I'd seen in the Alps, Pyrenees or high Himalaya, these were not familiar boulder palettes of lime or rust stain, nor ragged tatters hanging from trees, but deep gray cushions of delicate and intricate beauty, hitherto unknown to me. When wet they took on sponge-like qualities, but when dry (as I was to find a week later) they were delicate and brittle with tiny antlers woven into intense mattresses or cushions that settled on rock and boulder alike. Representatives of the arctic tundra (yet still far south of the Arctic Circle), for their very existence they required long months of harsh drying winds and snow cover, and then twenty-four hours of daylight. And rain. The rain that is the curse of the ambitious walker.

I studied, sniffed, and tasted lichens whose formal nomenclature I will probably never know, whose very existence is one of nature's miracles, whose secrets lie beyond my depths of perception. Bewitched by the extraordinary diversity of the world about me, I reeled in ignorance and wonder.

Could I exchange this ignorance for knowledge, would my sense of wonder be enhanced? I doubt it. For the blessings of this bad-weather day were every bit as rewarding as any sun-drenched morning. And no amount of knowledge could improve that.

A version of this story appeared in the July 2006 edition of *Loose Scree*.

[SPAIN]

THE FRAGRANCE OF THE HILLS

A press trip to a mountain region of which I knew next to nothing was squeezed between a hectic summer in the Alps and another Himalayan trek. For a few days in the autumn of 2004 I was introduced to a surprisingly remote and seemingly deserted land

of sun-baked sierras between Valencia and Alicante, which captured
my imagination and brought many rewards.

At midnight I sat naked to the waist on the balcony outside my room plucking grapes from an overhanging vine as the warmth and fragrance of Spain drifted through the valley. The rest of the old village of white walls and broken terracotta roofs lay huddled on a slope of sand-colored hills. Behind them could be seen the outline of mountains folded like sleeping dinosaurs against a backdrop of stars, their individual features lost in the darkness. In that darkness a dog barked somewhere far off. Then silence settled once more, for the cicadas were resting.

By day I'd walked past Moorish ruins that gave the landscape both identity and history. Among those ruins snails clung to stones once fashioned into doorways, while lizards zipped in staccato motion from shadow to light and back again. Stirring the air, black redstarts rushed in a frenzy across the ruins and were gone, leaving only the echoing beat of their feathers. As the sun burned from a cloudless sky, I'd scuffed the dust of a track through abandoned olive groves then, passing tiny-leaved holly oak, withered pine, and gorse, taken a trail that climbed towards a ridge of limestone, where a welcome breeze carried a potpourri of scents— curry plant, rosemary, mountain sage, and boxwood.

Up there, among sand-blasted spires and turrets, holes—some as big as a man—had been worn in the rock by thousands of years of erosion. Erosion spelt decay, and it was this, along with drought and desolation, that had driven men from this land that once had thrived not just with olive groves but with almond, vine, fig, and orange trees. Now the land was dry. There had been no rain since the spring, and the long weeks of summer had scorched or singed every plant. Down there, it was said, wild boar had been seen. Up on the ridge, I was told, a pair of Bonelli's eagle had been sighted, and golden eagle and griffon vultures sometimes worked the thermals. The land may be impoverished, as far as man was concerned, but nature contrived a brave reclamation.

Passing through one of the man-sized holes, I made a steep descent on loose rock into a pit of spiky plants and brambles, then headed out onto baked screes and a faint contouring path beneath a row of rocky fingers before climbing once more through a gully. This was followed by a scramble to reach a summit overlooking the remains of an old Moorish watchtower, where swifts gathered in preparation for their flight to Africa. The Moors knew what they were doing, for as a vantage point it was unbeatable. Although the mountain was modest in altitude, all the world, it seemed, was laid out below. In one direction dry shadowed *barrancos* were loud with the sound of crickets instead of waterfalls and mountain torrents; in another the sun dazzled on one of the far distant tower blocks of the Costa Blanca. Those buildings were another world away, another lifetime. An involuntary shudder expressed my feelings.

Down in the village, with night holding that alien world at bay, I plucked another grape from the vine crawling over my balcony and yet again caught a drift of fragrance from the cooling hills. My days here among the aromatic Valls de la Marina were filled with sensory experience. In a week's time I would be in the Himalaya trekking among lush foothills to the highest mountains on Earth, but for now I could bask in the fragrance of Spain and the gentle warmth of contentment. And that was more than enough for me.

LUNCHING WITH LIZARDS

Researching walking routes on behalf of a travel company gave me a week's introduction to Madeira in the spring of 2002. From the very first day I was enchanted by the island's natural beauty and abundant flora. I scrambled over its mountains, followed ancient levadas, splashed through ravines and wandered along the tops of great cliffs where seabirds wheeled and cried. And at the end of that week I knew I'd have to return. The lizards would make sure of that.

Taking a day off from exploring the mountainous heart of Madeira, I stretched out on the grass and inhaled the aromatic drift of a dozen exotic plants, the midday light dazzling in the water some 300 feet below. Just ahead the land narrowed to a pencil-sharp peninsula, and a single glance took in cliffs that fell abruptly on both the north and the south sides of the island. I'd already completed a morning's walk along those cliffs, and reckoned I could manage another in the afternoon—if I didn't fall asleep, that is, lulled by the swirl of the tide and lazy call of seabirds. But hunger gnawed, so I dug in my rucksack for a couple of bread rolls and a lump of cheese, and began a simple lunch.

Moments later a five-inch lizard appeared, testing the air to sample an alien smell. I dropped a crumb. The lizard approached, dabbed it with its tongue, appreciated the taste, attacked it with tiny jaws, then shook it, chewed, and swallowed. Hmm, tasted good.

Another crumb fell. The lizard pounced, turned it with its nose, took it in its mouth, and raced away. News spread fast: "There's free food on the clifftop."

A second lizard appeared—this one with a curious streak down its back; tongue darting, twitching, tasting. Then another, a sandy-brown fella with bandy legs and a dinosaur's tail. A third lizard appeared, and a fourth. Then there were nine or ten, of different sizes and varying shades, but all sharing a common hunger for bread and cheese. *My* bread and cheese.

Lounging in the grass, I barely moved as one creature after another scaled the north face of my rucksack, clambered over my water bottle, then onto my legs, up my arms, and across my shoulders. Lizards everywhere—or nearly everywhere—tongues dabbing for a crumb.

I began to laugh and the lizards froze. One cocked its head, another fell as my body shook, while a third—a six-inch reptile with bulging eyes—stared at me from my right shoulder and was not enamoured by what it saw. In a flash he was off, and although I didn't hear it, a cry must have gone out: "Make haste lads—it's a hooman."

Moments later I was alone on the clifftop with what was left of my lunch. But my appetite had gone with the lizards, so I broke the remains of my bread into tiny crumbs and wandered away. It was, after all, their clifftop, not mine. And they ought to be left in peace.

[TENERIFE]

ISLAND OF THE DRAGON TREE

Although I knew that Pico del Teide, the 12,198 foot volcano on Tenerife, was the highest mountain on Spanish territory, I hadn't expected to find such variety of wild landscapes when I arrived on the island early in 1989. Snow was dusting the ground at home, but the island was bathed in sunshine as each day we set out to sample its many natural features. The only downside to the experience was our guide, the owner of the company whose invitation had brought me there, and whose claim to know the island like the back of his hand was to prove false before even the second day was over.

Tenerife dispelled all my fears and expectations. Its reputation for booze-fueled revelers ensured it would not be my favored choice of destination, but an assignment to join a walking group to write a magazine feature was something different, and by the second day, and against all the odds, the island had won me over.

That second day's walk began in the far northeast, where a rocky spine clad in a veritable jungle of tree heathers and forests of laurel plunged to a drift of distant surf. A long tail of cloud streaked the hills early each morning, ensuring a lush green and damp landscape, so different from the barren moonscape of Las Cañadas, in the shadow of Pico del Teide, where we'd walked the day before.

On this second day we were taken to a remote restaurant on a cliff edge, where the wind hammered the cracked plaster and howled through the pan of the toilet—it was no place to spend five comfortable minutes, although it certainly kept the cubicle aired. Along the narrow spine beyond the restaurant curving bays of the south coast could be seen hundreds of feet below. The trail we took wound between ancient laurel trunks draped in Spanish moss, with huge ferns threatening to swallow the path.

The crest buckled, and we broke away to plunge out of the cool, moist greenery to blue views and sunshine, where tiny villages lay scattered like dice among ravines and terraced fields beneath. This was a coastline tinged with mystery—its black stacks and spires standing offshore in showers of spray, and the limitless sea beyond everything, furrowed with dark lines of the daily swell that told of the ocean's breathing.

Out of the wind, I dawdled and let the group get ahead, drawing deeply on a rich fusion of scents, listening to island sounds, recalling its volcanic origins.

As we headed down again, the temperature rose to summer while the calendar spoke still of winter. Prickly pear (without flower) and Canary bellflower (in bloom) marked the way; my legs brushed against a dozen different herbs that smeared the air with fragrance, but the handkerchief-sized terraces that were passed showed few signs of husbandry, despite the obvious fertility of the soil.

The village was El Draguillo, named for the dragon tree that stood on its outskirts. Almost smothered in prickly pear, El Draguillo was an orange-roofed throwback to a past era—an isolated hamlet two-thirds of the way down a mountain slope towards the sea, and apart for the yapping of unseen dogs you would have thought it deserted.

Not long after, I caught up with the group gazing in different directions while the leader and founder of the company that arranged the holiday stood red-faced and puzzled, trying to make sense of the map. This middle-aged Englishman had boasted that he'd been brought up on Tenerife and spent most of his life here. He knew all the paths, all the best views, all the finest restaurants and hotels; he'd walked everywhere, or so he claimed. I guessed he'd started his business with the misguided idea that arranging and leading walking holidays was an easy way to make a fortune. But within an hour of our meeting it was clear that he was not the most perceptive or discreet of men. He'd already alienated at least one of his guests and was now proving the lie to his claim to know the island like the back of his hand. He was lost. Well and truly lost, and his embarrassment was obvious.

Seeing me arrive, his eyes blazed as he thrust the map at me and barked, "You're a mountain man. You find the bloody way!"

The map was not the finest piece of cartography I'd seen, but it was all we had. But having studied my own copy at breakfast, and again a few minutes ago in order to learn the name of the village, I had a vague idea where we were. "Show me where we're due to meet the bus," I said. He did so, his finger shaking from embarrassment and anger; anger, I suspect, with himself, and I admit to feeling a little sorry for him. But only a little.

Confused at first by vegetation, the narrow trail soon became clear before vanishing again. Then it reappeared to take us on a switchback course over a series of shallow ravines, then steeply down to disappear under slithers of scree and black grit on the way to a stony beach, magnificent in its isolation. In whichever direction we looked, there was nothing of man, save that which had been washed up by the tides that came unhindered thousands of sea miles from the coast of North America. It was the perfect coastline, with neither pier nor jetty, no gentle cove of sand littered with sun worshippers, no donkey rides nor ice cream stalls. Just wave-lashed rocks and sentry-like stacks topped by gannets and a dazzle of spray. Cliffs hung tenuously above the tides; bays cut scoops from them, while elsewhere the green island fell to the sea.

"I'll take over now," said our leader with sudden confidence, snatching his map from me. "This way. Keep up." And he marched along the beach like a Victorian general leading his troops into battle.

[TURKEY]

▲

YOGURT WITH THE MATRIARCH

Turkey has some fine mountains—the Taurus, Cilo Sat, and Kaçkar ranges among them. Best known, of course, is Mount Ararat, the highest of them all at about 16,945 feet. Traditionally thought to be the final resting place of Noah's ark following the Great Flood, this dormant volcano rises out of a plain in eastern Turkey, with Armenia to the north, Iran to the east, and Iraq to the south. Having never been to Turkey before I was delighted to receive an invitation to travel there in 1990 and to make the ascent of Mount Ararat. It was an opportunity too good to resist.

The Kurdish guide allocated by the authorities for my ascent of Mount Ararat, to make sure I didn't stray off course and into military-sensitive areas, had been born on the slopes of the mountain, his parents being shepherds who moved their flock from *yayla* to *yayla* throughout the year. Tall and slim, with shiny black hair, dark eyes, and a mischievous grin, Mehmut chain-smoked his way to the summit, hands in pockets, and managing somehow to sing at the same time. There were moments as I was struggling to breathe when I could happily have murdered him.

But he endeared himself to me on the way to Camp One as we got to know one another. In difficult-to-understand pidgin English, and with extravagant hand gestures, he first regaled me with an imaginative history of the mountain, then took me to meet his family who had gathered their tents on a level patch of land flattened and blackened by the dung of scores of sheep and goats penned there overnight.

Inside a large brown goat-hair yurt his mother, a regal matriarch with hawk-like nose and sharp eyes, lounged against a pile of cushions fashioned into what could almost be called a throne. Dressed in a brilliant green blouse and voluminous skirts, fingers decorated with rings, and head shrouded in a cream-colored scarf tied with a cord, she was clearly a formidable woman. How old she might be was impossible to tell; her very appearance was a contradiction, for her skin had been furrowed by a lifetime of mountain weather, her voice rang with authority that allowed no interruption, but severity would melt in a second and give way to an open-mouthed smile that revealed the teeth of a Hollywood starlet.

Nephews, nieces, children, and grandchildren sat at her feet on a faded rug, and with a nod and a gesture from the matriarch in green, space was made for me, so I too sat at her feet like a humble ambassador come to pay his government's respects to the queen of a foreign land.

Visit a home in Europe and you'll be offered a cup of tea or coffee, or perhaps something stronger. But here in eastern Turkey at about 10,000 feet on the slopes of Mount Ararat, with the borders of Armenia, Iran, and Iraq not far off, a large, slightly rusting tin of yogurt was handed to me. I turned to my guide and raised an eyebrow. He smiled, flicked a cigarette out of the doorway, and indicated I should drink.

I looked down into the tin, then made another silent appeal to the guide. Drink? He nodded. I turned to the matriarch, whose eyes burned into my face. Those eyes spoke volumes—they needed no words to relay their message—but the starlet's teeth smiled, and with a sense of foreboding I looked once more into the warm contents of the tin in my hands.

Now I like yogurt. I have fresh, home-made yogurt with my breakfast cereal each morning. Straight from the fridge, my wife's yogurt has a pure creamy texture. It lies smooth in the dish; it's not yellowing, thick, lumpy, and moving. There are no goat hairs in my wife's yogurt; no livestock paddling from one side to the other. It has no alien flavors, no uninvited additions. This tin, however, held a cocktail of unwelcome mysteries.

On planning my ascent of Mount Ararat, yogurt had played no part. But guests in a foreign land have duties and responsibilities— so, aware of the matriarch's gaze, I swallowed hard, lifted the tin to my lips, closed my eyes . . . and thought of England.

• • •

THE GARDEN OF TEARS

Peru and the great chain of the Andes had long been near the top of my list of "must-visit" places. I'd read plenty of books, expedition reports and magazine features, and drooled over countless photographs of soaring peaks caked with snow and ice, tumbling glaciers, exotic plants, and a unique wildlife. At last, in 2000, the opportunity arose to go there with a trekking group and to write about it for a magazine. But before we began our trek we stopped off at Yungay at the foot of the mountain of Huascaran—or rather, where the town of Yungay used to be.

Huascaran was in a benevolent mood, with sunlight gleaming on snowfields that rose above a slim veil of cloud. At more than 22,000 feet, its status as the highest mountain in Peru was unchallenged. Towering what seemed but a short distance away, Huascaran was a regal monument of nature, a serene presence whose twin summits were divided by a deep saddle, from which a glacier hung in a motionless cascade. The dome of Huascaran Sur climbed to the right of the saddle, Norte on the left, with a bare cliff of granite revealed beneath a pelmet of ice. Below the cloud's veil the lower slopes faded into anonymity, concealed by a ridge spur outlined with trees.

Around me in the garden at the foot of Huascaran flowers bloomed, their fragrance stirred by midday warmth and a soft breeze. A few butterflies drifted; green rafts of lilies floated in a small pond. The mountain smiled a benediction; as a backdrop it seemed both majestic and protective, a trusty neighbor.

Yet Huascaran is anything but trusty and protective. In 1962 a hanging glacier broke free from its northern flank, engulfing the small town of Ranrahica and ending the lives of four thousand of its residents.

Worse was to come.

Mid-afternoon on Sunday 31 May 1970, Peru suffered a major earthquake measuring 7.8 on the Richter scale. About 90 miles from the epicenter, Huascaran shuddered like an enormous blanc-mange. Moments later the west face of the north peak shed an esti-mated 80 million cubic feet of rock and ice which, together with a mass of glacial silt, mud, snow, and earth sped towards the town of Yungay. Within three minutes the town, and 18,000 inhabitants, lay buried. Yungay and its people had ceased to exist.

A little over thirty years later I stood in the memorial garden that covers the site of that lost town, mesmerized by the horror and reminded of the impermanence of all things. There was no substance to the poet's eternal hills—their fragility had been exposed—and among the flowers an uneasy silence was disturbed by a fluster of excited birds that chattered in the shrubs, unaware that this was a garden of tears.

With slow, reverential footsteps I moved through the garden, trying to imagine the fear that would have gripped the good folk of Yungay that Sunday afternoon – what were their final words; the last thoughts that crowded their minds? Huascaran had always been there as a major backdrop to their lives. They would have known all its moods, wondered at the beauty of its alpenglow, shuddered at the distant roar of its avalanches. But on that May Sunday three decades ago, preceded by a wall of wind, a mighty cloud of doom would have taken the mountain from view, and with it their town, their families and their friends.

Other than a small pile of masonry and the wreckage of a bus that lies mangled, twisted, and crushed, all that remains of the lost town are four palm trees. Everything else belongs to the recent past; anything pre-1970 has been obliterated.

I looked up at a towering statue of Christ, dazzling white with arms outstretched, and facing Huascaran as if to hold back any repetition of the mountain's unspeakable act of betrayal, and there whispered a prayer for the dead.

That evening my tent was pitched alongside those of my group in a meadow by the lakes of Llanganuco. Andean geese cackled from the lakeside while a wooly herd of alpaca grazed nearby. As the light faded I heard a bird call. Streams ran clear from ice-bound mountains that blocked the valley, and when I strolled to the lakeshore to welcome the oncoming darkness, I knew again that old familiar tingle of excitement born of anticipation of new mountains to explore. But this was mingled with sorrow, too, for lives cut short on the other side of the mountain.

Huascaran had much to answer for.

[PERU]

▲

ALPAMAYO DREAMING

Alpamayo, the name is as graceful as the mountain—an elegant pyramid that teased us throughout our journey among the high peaks of Peru's Cordillera Blanca in 2000. Some mountains show themselves day after day as you trek towards them—Kangchenjunga is a prime example. Others, like Mont Blanc, treat those who walk the Tour of Mont Blanc to an ever-changing prospect. But not Alpamayo. It refused to reveal itself until we'd gazed on other Andean giants and crossed several high passes. Only then would the ultimate temptress grant the view we'd hoped for. But it was worth the wait.

At almost 16,400 feet the pass was bleak and rocky, but the mountains on show made it much less of a moonscape than the basin out of which we'd just climbed. Once again I'd hoped for Alpamayo, but cloud streamers denied us its summit, leaving only Santa Cruz momentarily free. It was no place to linger, for a bullying wind threatened to dislodge anything not tethered down. Small stones were being lifted and tossed at us, and dust devils spiraled up the mountainside to discolor any exposed flesh, get caught in eyes and nostrils, and knot our hair. The fourteen laden burros were ahead, already slithering down a slope of grit and scree and adding to the dust. With them our crew of five weather-tanned Quecha men and one woman were undaunted by the wind, the dust or the gradient, and they gradually drew away from us.

We caught up with them where they'd stopped to eat among a nest of rocks and tussock grass that deflected the wind. From there a cobalt-blue lake could be seen trapped among moraines at the foot of Alpamayo; all around her ice-crusted peaks were wrapped in shawls of mist and wind-borne snow, as was she. Alpamayo was the ultimate temptress, and the less we could see of her, the more we desired.

Our camp for the next two nights was in a rocky meadow through which a glacial torrent thrashed by day, but it was almost silenced by a double glazing of ice by night. Nearby, a patch of sand-like glacier flour edged our meadow, and once the burros had been freed of their loads, they rolled on their backs, legs kicking with joy in a flurry of dust.

It had taken eight days and a series of high passes to get here. Each one had opened a window onto the glories of the Cordillera Blanca; each night had found us in a valley with mountains to savor. We'd gazed on Huascaran, Huandoy, Pisco, and majestic Chacraraju, listened to avalanches falling from multi-peaked Pucahirca, and studied the ice crests of Talliraju. Only Alpamayo had been missing from our tally of giants. But this camp would be different, for it was obvious now that our seducer, wrapped still in clouds, was standing at the head of the stream. Surely she would reveal all before long?

Here in the valley the wind eased, but rain fell as evening drew in. Then the rain stopped and a bitter chill gripped the camp. Pulling on my down jacket I crawled out of the tent to discover cloud-mountains stained by the setting sun drifting across the skies. As I stood transfixed a movement caught my attention, and I spied a fox with a blue-gray coat and long tail nosing among rocks near where the burros were tethered. I watched him for a minute or two, then turned and looked upvalley, and my throat went dry. For there was Alpamayo in all her glory at last, rising above a turmoil of glaciers—an exquisite, perfectly formed pyramid, sharp as a pencil and unbelievably graceful. No clouds intruded. Clad only in ice and snow she was all I'd imagined her to be.

Weak-legged with admiration, I sank onto a rock and gazed up at that cone of perfection. Her summit, 5,000 feet above the stream, appeared to sway in a jet-stream wind unknown down here, where frost would soon cover the grass and stiffen our tents. Reality and the gathering darkness were dismissed from my mind. I gave no thought for tomorrow; had no anticipation of dawn's welcome light that would bleed on that snow and ice in the morning, nor any care that a full day would be spent gaining higher vantage points from which to study her features. All that belonged to the future. For now Alpamayo, reckoned by many to be the world's most beautiful mountain, had set me dreaming.

AFTERTHOUGHT

I've been lucky. It was never my intention to dedicate the most active years of my life to producing guidebooks. That was not a career choice, but fate stepped in, and before I knew it I was spending weeks and months in some of the world's most dramatic wild landscapes. Walking, trekking, climbing, *living* every moment.

Creating this book of recollections has been an indulgence. Most of the stories came to life at the start of a day's work, or in the evening after I'd already spent seven or eight hours writing. Often I'd been working on a guidebook, and describing a route over a mountain pass had stirred memories that brought that particular moment into sharp focus. Eager to relive the experience once more I'd write it down. More often than not the words came easily—a torrent of words pouring like a mountain stream as an incident that had lain dormant maybe for years was suddenly given new life, resurrected by the necessity to revisit a time and a place far removed from the world outside my window.

Recreating special moments from my years among the mountains is a continuing joy. That is one of the gifts of memory. We may strive to live *in* the moment, *for* the moment, but real joy can be extracted from those experiences whenever we choose to trawl through the past, and we can do that a thousand times over with a single experience.

Tom Longstaff, one of the greatest of the early Himalayan mountaineer-explorers, once decreed that "happiness is most often found by those who have learned to live in every moment of the present, [and] none has such prodigal opportunities of attaining that as the traveller." He went on to say that "attainment of a set objective is but a secondary matter, the traveller should not anticipate the journey's end."

Longstaff's "traveller" was a mountaineer. But all who go to the mountains have abundant opportunities to gather a harvest of memories worth reliving. Happily there's no need to be a top-grade climber tackling the latest major vertical challenge, nor even to trek the longest or toughest routes, for with an eye for beauty and the ability to absorb the wonders of the world around you, enrichment comes from simply being there.

I hope that message comes across in some of the stories in this book, and will inspire you to gather a harvest of experience and memory to underline the truth that life is a gift to be treasured and not wasted on "if only . . . ".

GLOSSARY

abri	small stone shelter found in Corsica and the French Pyrenees
altopiano	high-altitude plateau in the Italian mountains
barranco	ravine (*Spanish*); sometimes used to describe a dried river bed
bharal	so-called "blue sheep" of the Himalaya
cabane pastorale	basic herder's hut in French mountains
cairns	a man-made stack of stones, often erected as markings for hiking trails
chaarpi	a toilet or latrine in the Himalaya
chamois	an agile short-horned goat-antelope (Rupicapra rupicapra) of the Alpine regions
chang	home-brewed beer made from corn, rice or millet in Nepal or Tibet
chhu	river (*Bhutanese*)
chorten	a Buddhist monument, like an elaborate cairn
choughs	a crow-like bird
chuba	traditional Tibetan dress worn by Sherpa women
daal bhat	staple meal of Nepal: boiled rice with lentil sauce
didi	older sister—but the term is often used by trekkers to address a female lodge owner

djellaba	long hooded outer garment worn by Berber men in the Atlas Mountains
doko	woven conical basket used for carrying loads
dzong	a monastery fortress built to protect Bhutan's valleys from invasion
forcella	mountain pass (Italian)
gardien	person in charge of a mountain refuge
gîte d'étape	(*abbr* gîte)—a privately-owned hostel
gompa	a Buddhist monastery
ibex	wild mountain goat (Capra ibex) found in many Alpine regions
izard	the Pyrenean chamois, slightly smaller than its Alpine counterpart (see above)
kani	an elaborate archway decorated with Buddhist motifs
kessel	a deep hollow found in the limestone Alps
kira	traditional dress worn by Bhutanese women
klettersteig	the German word for a via ferrata (see below)
kora	the circuit of a religious building or symbol performed by devout Buddhists
levada	irrigation channel in the highlands of Madeira
mani	from the Buddhist prayer "Om mani padme hum"; it is carved on stones and printed on silk or cloth for prayer flags
namaste	traditional greeting; it means "I salute the god within you"
portillon	a high mountain pass in the Spanish Pyrenees
puja	Buddhist devotion; a puja room is the part of a Buddhist home reserved for prayer
Pyrénéisme	an emotional attachment to the Pyrenees that goes beyond mountaineering

refuge/refugio	a mountain hut in the Alps or Pyrenees
saeter	herder's cabin or seasonal farm in the mountains of Norway
salamander	a tailed amphibious creature found in the Alps and Pyrenees
sirdar	person in charge of local support crew for trekking or mountaineering expedition
soldanella	the tassel-flowered alpine snowbell, one of the first flowers to appear in springtime, often seen in a patch of melting snow
stupa	hemispherical Buddhist structure, like a large *chorten*
thanka	a religious painting, usually created on silk fabric
tikka	mark of blessing pressed on the forehead of a Hindu
tsampa	roasted barley flour
via ferrata	literally an "iron path" consisting of fixed cables, ladders, metal stanchions and even bridges to aid the ascent of steep cliffs—best known in the Italian Dolomites but now being developed throughout the Alps
yayla	the camp of semi-nomadic Kurdish shepherds on Mount Ararat